MW00780136

Crossing the Jordan

On Judaism, Islam, and the West

Crossing the Jordan
On Judaism, Islam, and the West

David Solway

Published by New English Review Press
a subsidiary of World Encounter Institute
PO Box 158397
Nashville, Tennessee 37215
&
27 Old Gloucester Street
London, England, WC1N 3AX

Cover art and design by Kendra Mallock

ISBN: 978-1-943003-92-1
Library of Congress Control Number: 2023946433

First Edition

NEW ENGLISH REVIEW PRESS
newenglishreview.org

For George Koch, editor, C2C Journal
and
Saul Kahn, landsman

CONTENTS

INTRODUCTORY NOTE

A number of these essay chapters have appeared in earlier versions in scattered journals. Many are no longer archived, which prompted me to revive them in contemporary garb. An earlier version of the "Philistine Times" appeared in my *The Boxthorn Tree* and it seemed appropriate to include it here, if only to lighten the overall tone. The title chapter featured in *C2C Journal* to commemorate Israel's Diamond Jubilee in 2023. *Crossing the Jordan* is the companion volume to *The Boxthorn Tree*, published by Freedom Press Canada in 2012.

Beat your plowshares into swords, and your pruning hooks into spears: let the weak say, I am strong.
Book of Joel, *3:10*

1

CELEBRATING ISRAEL'S DIAMOND JUBILEE

Behold, the ark of the covenant of the Lord of all the earth passeth over before you into the Jordan. —Joshua, 3:11

Yom Ha'Atzmaut marks the establishment of the modern state of Israel on May 14, 1948, the day on which David Ben-Gurion, the *de facto* leader of the Jewish community in Palestine, publicly read the Israeli Declaration of Independence. The Jewish people, he announced, "reclaimed the wilderness, revived the language, built cities and villages" and revived a state with "explicit international recognition of ... their right to reconstitute their National Home." As Israel now prepares to celebrate its Diamond Jubilee, signifying 75 turbulent years dating from the invasion of five Arab armies on the *very day* of its induction into the community of nations, it is well to remember the words of the prophet Isaiah that Israel was to be "a light unto the Nations" (*Isaiah* 49:6).

Much of the world begs to differ. Israel is the one nation on Earth whose right to exist is widely questioned and threatened. It is the disproportionate target of the United Nations Human Rights Council which devotes many of its sessions to attacking the Jewish state, approving in 2022 alone 15 anti-Israel resolutions promoted by the Palestinians while giving some of the world's most scandalous human rights violators—China, Saudi Arabia, Turkey, Venezuela, Qatar—a Get Out of Jail Free card. Israel has been subjected to unfairness by the European Union, a worldwide boycott, divestment and sanctions (BDS) campaign, and the vicious defamation of Israel Apartheid Weeks hosted on our morally debased university campuses. The *Washington Free Beacon* reports that President Joe Biden's Administration is increasing U.S. aid to the Palestinian Authority as it pursues its "pay-to-slay" terrorist program.

As Lincoln Brown writes in *PJ Media*, "One would think that in a supposedly-enlightened age, the naked hatred and prejudices of the past would have already been consigned to history. But of course, this is not an enlightened age. People are motivated by stereotypes, rhetoric, and a situation in Israel that they do not fully understand or care to research." The ideology of the left continues to demonize Israel as a racist and conquistador nation that should be delegitimized—a state beyond the pale, to cite the title of Robin Shepherd's book on the subject. Meanwhile, its Muslim neighbors, particularly in the West Bank and Gaza, have vowed to physically erase Israel from the map of the world, launching terrorist attacks—as, for example, on January 27, on February 10, and counting—firing rockets at its civic centers, and pursuing their version of the Final Solution. Every period of relative quiet is routinely described as a "lull" in the hostilities.

The propaganda assault on Israel is merely another species of terrorism, the contemporary form of the age-old anti-Jewish pogrom, as Bat Ye'or has persuasively argued in *Eurabia: The Euro-Arab Axis,* and *Islam and Dhimmitude: Where Civilizations Collide.* Obviously, bigotry and baseless aspersion are never openly admitted. Rather, for antisemites and anti-Zionists, Israel is regarded as a geopolitical irritant, a historical mistake, a garrison kingdom, an artificial construct that should never have been established, however validly and legally. Does the 1967 UN Resolution 242, guaranteeing "the sovereignty, territorial integrity and political independence of every State in the area and their right to live in peace within secure and recognized boundaries," have no juridical force? (As is to be expected, the UN is currently violating its own principles.)

For Islam, Israel is an interloper in the region, despite the indisputable historical fact that Israel and Judah predate the Arab occupation of the Holy Land by more than a thousand years. Surah 17, ayah 1 of the *Koran* mentions the pre-existing Temple at Jerusalem; indeed, it mentions the presence of the Jews and Moses in the Holy Land multiple times (e.g.: 2:47-48; 9:30; 2:83; 3:110; 3:199; 7:159; 2:62; 22:40; 5:5; 7:145). Jerome Verlin in *Israel 3000 Years* tabulates in exacting detail the historical presence of the *Yishuv*, or homeland community, "in the four holy cities of Jerusalem, Safed, Tiberias and Hebron, as well as in the rural grassroots of the land." No matter. For the so-called "realist" school of international relations—see John Mearsheimer and Stephen Walt's *The Israel Lobby and U.S. Foreign Policy*—Israel is a political liability and therefore not entitled to American and international sympathy and concern.

Moreover, Israel is by no means a great power. Its current population of 9.4 million (including its Muslim citizens) makes it by normal census standards sparsely populated, and it covers about as much territory as Wales or New Jersey. As former mayor of New York Ed Koch reputedly said, one "might need a magnifying glass to see Israel" in a World Atlas since it could easily "disappear in the crease of a page." In the larger scheme of things, presumably, its absence would scarcely be noticed.

And yet it can be argued that Israel's existence is an absolute necessity. It is, to begin with, a haven for the Jewish people from the world's ancient antipathy. As Leonard Cohen sang in one of his most moving songs, "Dance me through the panic 'til I'm gathered safely in," a lyric version of Moses' Song in *Deuteronomy* 32 in which Jacob is led from "the waste howling wilderness" and kept in "the apple of the Lord's eye."

Israel is a testimony to historical continuity and cultural memory in an age of temporal dissipation, a sort of "Benedict Option" for Jews—although a decidedly well-armed one, with stealth fighter jets, nuclear missiles and submarines. It is a sign of what is possible when a people gather together and pool their intelligence, courage, obstinacy and talent to create a vibrant pluralist democracy in the midst of ignorance and barbarism. Israel is a country that gives more to the world than many other countries, excelling in the fields of science, technology, medicine, agriculture, and energy. Israel has more Nobel laureates in absolute terms than China, and more hi-tech start-ups *per capita* than anywhere else on the planet.

Among the many inventions and discoveries coming out of Israel, we note: the PillCam (endoscopy system), the flexible stent, the computer firewall, the ICQ Instant Messenger, the collaborative development of the first cell phone, the world's first USB drive, desert irrigation (Netafim), Mobileye (tiny vehicle cameras to warn of hazards), ReWalk (battery-powered exoskeleton), the smart watch, Duali-Q (radiology software), nano-magnets (to restore damaged nerve cells), and most recently a 23-pound, cost-effective, fuel-efficient car engine that just might be the wave of the future. George Gilder's *The Israel Test* and Dan Senor and Saul Singer's *Start-Up Nation* have made luminously clear the extent of Israel's innovative genius from which the entire world has profited, which does not prevent the Jewish state from being considered a pariah among the nations. Yet the renaissance is real.

What we seem to be witnessing, as Eric Nelson reminds us in *The Hebrew Republic: Jewish Sources and the Transformation of European Political Thought*, is a contemporary reprise of the emergence of vast quantities of ground-breaking Hebraica texts and documents in the late 16th to mid-17th centuries, a revival which "transformed European literature and criticism, medicine and science, theology and ecclesiology, and philosophy and law, and (the principles of) political thought." The scholarly term for the historical embodiment of these materials is the *republica Hebraeorum*, which profoundly influenced among others John Locke and his meditations on representative government that underlie the political organization of the liberal West.

Of course, Israeli politics soon became and remains splintered among innumerable fractious parties, a misfortune of which Locke would not have approved, though the country remains a robust, if tempestuous, democracy. Contemporary Israel is also an object lesson in how to manage a sound economy, running an engine with almost no gap in the output curve (although it had wallowed for several decades under social-democratic mismanagement). And it is, of course, the spearhead of the democratic West in the war against Islamic terror, receiving and resisting the brunt of the theo-imperialist onslaught against Western institutions, interests and, indeed, long-term survival. The Islamic writ is found in ayat like *Koran* 9:33 in which Allah sends forth his prophet "to make the true faith supreme over all religions."

Those who study the history of civilization and who are disturbed or fascinated by the specter of decline exhibited by our own, will find Israel important for another reason. As I contended in *The Big Lie* and in a *C2C Journal* essay, it is difficult to repress the suspicion that ominous forces are working toward the demise of Judeo-Christian civilization. And I would hazard that many people in the ordinary walks of life are troubled by an inchoate premonition that something has gone terribly wrong with Western culture, governed by a political elite without moral convictions and educated by an academic elite without scholarly scruples, a charge convincingly documented in Ibn Warraq's masterful volume, *Defending the West*.

Many Western academics and intellectuals, Warraq writes, argue "that Western civilization is culturally, intellectually, and spiritually defective." Quite the contrary. "Western civilization is good for the world," having given it the principles of liberty and individual dignity, "the whole edifice of modern science ... the symphony and the novel ... the Red Cross, Doctors Without Borders," international aid, universal literacy and economic prosperity.

The "hostility to the West and Israel," Warraq concludes, is a "shameful betrayal" of the ideals inherited from the Greeks and the Bible. The classical principles of democracy, the Enlightenment and scientific investigation, the Ten Commandments and the Christian Gospels form the basis of Judeo-Christian civilization, which must be defended against those who derogate the gifts of freedom, individualism, energy and inventiveness with which it has endowed the world.

As physicist Stephen Meyer points out in *The Return of the God Hypothesis*, the advancement of human reason and scientific investigation developed only in the Judeo-Christian West, especially after the Christian Reformation in the 15th and 16th centuries and common access to the vernacular (non-Latin) Scriptures. This implied that the individual was able to use his own judgment instead of relying on authority and that "human beings could attain insight into the workings of the natural world," interrogating nature "using systematic experimental methods." For all its life-enhancing donations to mankind, however, the Judeo-Christian West is not only being attacked from outside, but is being dismantled piece by piece by internal forces, by its own *nomenklatura* and internecine defectors, the political cruft of our day.

In the present context of doubt and apprehension,

Israel, a testament to the singular, historical Western amalgam of science, democracy and communion, tells us who and what we are, that is, assuming we are interested in recognizing our own features. It constitutes a catechism for the West, a trial of values and a test of honor and principle—a test which the West appears to be failing. For the cherubs of political correctness and the fantasists among the intelligentsia cannot abide what Israel ideally exemplifies: vigilance in the face of aggression, the commitment to a genuine historic purpose and the virtue of unapologetic self-affirmation. They hate Israel because Israel stands as both living refutation of their self-hatred and physical resistance to their program of civilizational destruction.

Il Foglio journalist, culture critic and author Giulio Meotti persuasively argues that, "There is in fact only one Western country according to all democratic, cultural, social, civil and economic indexes, which has been going against the [disintegration] trend for years: Israel." Meotti notes that, "Half of Israelis are *Mizrahi* and they tend to be more traditional and less 'wokiste'" than those drawn from Western countries. Meotti quotes Nobel Prize literature laureate Saul Bellow, who wrote, "In this restless hour, the civilized world seems tired of its own civilization ... Israelis have something to teach the world." If Western nations, mired in ideological ruin, wish to survive, Meotti continues, they "must learn from this small Jewish country under existential threat where the self-hatred that runs through all Western societies is held in check by religious roots," by faith, fertility, family and a realistic attitude to a volatile world.

This is not to suggest that Israel is without blemish or that it has not been partially infected by the contemporary Western proneness to false hope and political myopia. The *Oslo travesty* (which sought to gain recognition of Israel in return for allowing a Palestinian state, but actually sounded the prelude to the Second Intifada), the disengagement from Gaza, the destabilizing Israeli left with its spurious ecumenism and subversive media outlets like *Haaretz*, and the "peace process" mirage are examples of such lapses. The recent aggressive protests against Prime Minister Benjamin Netanyahu's efforts to reform a hard-core, self-appointing, leftist Supreme Court, which regularly thwarts the will of right-leaning governments, is, to quote military and security professional Ben Kerido in *The Western Journal*, "a shocking contradiction of Israeli cultural values."

In the same vein, Melanie Phillips remarks that Netanyahu is reacting against the anti-democratic rule of an interventionist judicial activism, a system in which "judges have substituted politics and ideology for law," which has created a troubling breach between the autonomous dispensation of justice and the proper functioning of a duly elected government. Meanwhile,

Israeli commentator Caroline Glick recently reported that, "Israel has found itself in the midst of a simultaneous and coordinated assault [with] terror attacks countrywide and rocket volleys from Gaza, Lebanon and Syria."

In an April 10, 2023 speech, delivered in a time of public unrest, Netanyahu reminded the public that Hezbollah, Hamas and Iran (probably soon to be armed with nuclear weapons; it already has the ballistic missiles to deliver them) believe they can attack Israel with impunity. A punching bag does not win a boxing match. If the prevailing mindset does not change, 1973, the year in which Israelis almost lost their country, may happen again.

No less distressing, Israel's embrace of the Covid-19/vaccine narrative and coercive mandates, clandestinely serving as a data-sharing petri dish for the noxious Pfizer experiment, is an egregious or at any rate a stupid and unscrupulous act. Former Chair of Medical Microbiology at Mainz University Dr. Sucharit Bhakdi was in his rights when he excoriated the Israeli government for signing a ten-year agreement with Pfizer. Like any nation on the planet, Israel has its share of gonifs, opportunists and sell-outs. For Islam and diehard Israel-haters, the entire nation is perceived as a collection of such reprobates and often vilified as "evil." This is pure *treif*. What we call "evil," however problematic a notion, is a human faculty, attribute or vice.

Interestingly, in *The Varieties of Religious Experience*,

William James associates evil with the concept of "dirt," which he defines as "matter out of place." Drawing from James' insight, anthropologist Mary Douglas in *Purity and Danger*, her landmark study of the concepts of pollution and taboo, analyzes how rules of purity constitute an organizing element in culture, setting off order from chaos, the acceptable from the improper, the affiliated from "matter out of place." Jews, especially, are seen as "socially ambiguous," their real offence felt as always having been "outside the formal structures of society and the symbols by which it organizes itself."

Israel came to be regarded as *political matter out of place*, threatening the unity, coherence and order of the world, as if such were a fact rather than a fiction. It seems more appropriate to say it is not Israel but the anti-Zionist and anti-Jewish conceptual world, pursuing a duplicitous program of ideological apartheid against the Jewish state, that is itself septic, matter out of place—or perhaps better, *spirit out of place*. The fact is that Israel's cadastral address, as we will shortly see, is also its rightful and authentic home. For despite the calumny and dishonesty to which it is regularly subjected, Israel is the one place where Jews, even the unruly and the dissident left, are truly not out of place.

> *For too much truth, at first sight, ne'er attracts*
> —George Gordon, Lord Byron, *Don Juan*, Canto XI

Israel is accused in many quarters of having

"cleansed" Palestine of its indigenous inhabitants and replaced them on the land, a canard of the first magnitude. What such indictments fail to take into account is that even after numerous historical expulsions, Jews have always been present in the Holy Land. Douglas Petrovich's riveting archeological and epigraphical study *Origin of the Hebrews*, succeeding the equally engrossing *The World's Oldest Alphabet*, documents the Egyptian Captivity (or Sojourn) of the Israelites between 1876-1446 BC, latterly under the pharaohs Amenhotep II and Thutmoses III. The Exodus, the crossing of the Red Sea and later of the Jordan River would have occurred shortly afterward, the latter conventionally dated to 1406 BC, marking the traditional 40 years of wandering in the wilderness.

Severing the Jews' millennia-old connection to the land is integral in the contemporary campaign to delegitimize Israel. The tenurial claim of the Jewish people to the land of Israel is an indefeasible one, however, based on a founding scripture, a millennial hereditament and a continuous presence, further ratified by the genetic evidence of the *Cohen Modal Haplotype* pointing toward a common ancestor dating back to the approximate time of Aaron and Moses. (See also, among many such studies, the *American Journal of Human Genetics*, 2003, treating of Y-chromosome evidence for the origin of Ashkenazi Levites.)

Conversely, as Joan Peters has indisputably shown in her magisterial *From Time Immemorial*, sifting through mountains of data, census statistics, official reports, internal memoranda, travel narratives and archival material, the Palestinians are, to a considerable extent, a loose aggregate of historically recent settlers and migrants to the area. (Even the term "Palestine" is not a Muslim but a Roman designation, an administrative department renamed by the emperor Hadrian in the 2nd Century AD from Judaea to Syria Palaestina.) Peters' findings are reinforced by the Rev. James Parkes' meticulous study *Whose Land?*, where he reiterates that "there was no such thing historically as a 'Palestinian Arab,' and there was no feeling of unity among 'the Arabs' of this newly defined area until modern times."

The so-called Palestinian Nationality was fabricated in the 1960s by the Soviets and Yasser Arafat as the Palestinian Liberation Organization, or PLO. Indeed, Zahir Muhsein of the Palestinian National Council told the Dutch newspaper Trouw in 1977 that, "The Palestinian people does not exist ... Only for political and tactical reasons do we speak today about the existence of a Palestinian people ... to oppose Zionism." (The article is now almost impossible to locate, but we can find Muhsein's admission on YouTube, Enterprise-Record, Daniel Pipes, an important article by Arabist Robert Spencer, and other venues.) Yasser Arafat himself, in the authorized political biography written by Alan Hart, affirmed that the "Palestinian people have no national identity." Arafat intended to *confer* identity "through conflict with Israel." This did not prevent Arafat from referring to himself as a native Palestinian though he was born in Egypt.

British census reports during the Mandatory period of 1922-1948, seeking to reduce the importance of the Jewish claim to the land, were regularly falsified to create the impression of a massive and original Palestinian presence. Data assembled from several credible sources, relying on economic developments, extrapolated migratory flows, imputation theory and growth rate differentials, as reported in *The Middle East Quarterly* ("The Smoking Gun," Winter 2003), identify a substantial early 20th century flow of illegal Arab immigration into Mandatory Palestine from South Sinai, Trans-Jordan and Syria.

Examining the documents at the disposal of historians, commentator Daniel Grynglas concluded that, "95.7% of present-day Palestinians are clearly those Arabs and their descendants who migrated to Israel between 1831 and 2015." The claim that Palestinians "are the indigenous people of Israel and that most of the present Palestinian Arabs have lived in these lands since time immemorial is a total fraud." Similarly, in the essay collection *Ottoman Palestine 1800-1914*, social historian Gad Gilbar attributes the urban growth of the Arab population largely to "immigrants from outside Palestine," *whereas the Jewish presence in the Holy Land is longstanding and inherent.*

It is evident, then, that a significant number of "Palestinians" migrated into the Holy Land from the surrounding Arab countries, mainly from present-day Syria and Lebanon while still part of the Ottoman Empire, which were used as a bulwark against raiding Bedouin tribes. The Arab late arrivals after the Ottoman Empire's breakup were subsequently dubbed "Palestinians," as were the Jews who lived there. The fact that the "Palestinians" have no stories, no texts, no coins, no relics, no historically verified muniments, whereas Israel is replete with stories, memorial scriptures and artifacts from pre-Biblical times and possesses a calendar that dates to 5783, is dispositive. New archeological finds attesting to a millennial Jewish presence—from small but revelatory artifacts to elaborate public facilities—occur with corroborating regularity.

Historian Bruce Thornton in *The Wages of Appeasement* justly points out that "the professed concern for the dispossessed Palestinians" is a pretext "based on an Orwellian rewrite of history that erases the 3,000 year presence of Jews in the Holy Land and makes the descendants of conquerors, occupiers, and immigrants the rightful possessors." As jurist and former Attorney General of Canada Irwin Cotler wrote on the occasion of Israel's 60th anniversary, Israel "is the aboriginal homeland of the Jewish people across space and time and overlaps with the State of Israel ... as a political and juridical entity ...; it is, in international legal terms, a successor state to the biblical, or aboriginal, Jewish kingdoms."

As well, the late Roger Scruton in *The West and the Rest* confirms with much supporting evidence that, "Israel has transformed itself into a nation-state by allying a historical national identity with an existing territorial jurisdiction" to become, not a "Zionist entity," as Arab propaganda has it, but a legal entity with a genuinely accountable government. This is buttressed by the instrument of international law behind the League of Nations Mandate applying to the territory in dispute and pursuant to the successor UN Constitution that undertakes to abide by its predecessor's obligations and mandate agreements. It is pertinent to note that during the time of the British Mandate, the biblical term *Eretz Israel*, "Land of the People of Israel," was one of the territory's official names.

Regrettably, the likelihood of a just and lasting peace remains slender. Neither has it ever been satisfactorily explained why Israel must conclude a peace on terrorist terms or submit to the pressures of the surrounding Arab states which launched the wars they subsequently lost. Since when do culpable losers dictate terms? As statesman Abba Eban said of the Six Day War of 1967, "This is the first war in history which has ended with the victors suing for peace and the vanquished calling for unconditional surrender."

Is there a single country in the world that *willfully* returns territory captured in wars started by another country, when the defeated country still openly lusts for the other's destruction and refuses to make peace? This folly *might* be thinkable only if negotiations could be expected to bear genuine fruit. A durable peace cannot be based on the shimmer of a consensual mirage.

We recall that Israel withdrew from Lebanon and was rewarded with an armed Hezbollah entrenched on its northern borders and conducting regular incursions, kidnappings, shelling and rocket attacks, eventually provoking the war of summer 2006. When Israel withdrew from Gaza, it reaped a continuous barrage of rocket and mortar attacks on its southern villages and cities. We recall, too, that the Arabs and the Palestinians have refused to accept a two-state solution on four separate occasions: 1917 (the Balfour Declaration), 1937 (the Peel Commission), 1947 (the UN partition proposal) and 2000 (Camp David and Taba). U.S. President Bill Clinton's last-ditch bridge proposals were also rejected by the Palestinian side of the table.

Israel's present borders, as well as Judea and Samaria (aka the West Bank), comprise the historic and *legal* home of the Jewish people, a fact conveniently brushed aside. (The Golan Heights were admittedly not part of Israel but were legitimately taken in defensive action and are geographically critical to Israel's survival.) The historical truth is that the Balfour Declaration for the first time established a *political unit* called Palestine while recognizing that there already existed a historic Jewish right. The binding dispensations of international law, beginning with the Sykes-Picot Agreement of 1916 and culminating in Article 80 of the UN Charter, recognize and provide for Israeli settlement in Samaria and Judea—the so-called "occupied territories" —as part of Mandated Palestine, later captured by Israel as the spoils of a defensive war.

As Therese Zrihen-Dvir writes in *FrontPage Magazine*, those who accuse Israel of allegedly occupying territories that do not belong to it "position the heavy load of illegitimacy on the Jews' backs." The fact is, as the historical record proves, "Israel has only taken back what is rightfully his." Yet it has now become politically detrimental to pursue the issue and, in the name of an eventual, if unlikely, peace, much of the land in question will doubtlessly have to be formally ceded, with the exception of the cuticle around Jerusalem, a defensive wedge of the Jordan valley to ensure at least a minimum of strategic depth, and a handful of strategically-placed settlements, Palestinian violence notwithstanding.

The tiny state of Israel is like a postage stamp on a letter sent by a celestial syndic, seen through an anagogical lens as a mystical interpretation of distant events or scriptural exegesis. But there can be no denying that since its founding it has embodied an ideal of heroism, determination, enterprise, ancestral spirit and renewal rare, if not unprecedented, in the annals of modern statehood. The word "Israel" means "he who wrestles with God"

(*Genesis* 35:10) or in laic terms, the struggle and trial to prove oneself.

In this respect, Israel is like no other nation on earth. For this reason, the narrow slice of land between the Jordan River and the Mediterranean Sea is a kind of litmus strip for the civilization of which it is an intrinsic yet disparate part, to ascertain whether that civilization is viable or deficient, strong or weak, resilient or bankrupt, capable of integrity or inwardly corroded by spiritual indifference and intellectual corruption. In other words, *the way in which the West responds to Israel and its ongoing predicaments serves as an infallible indication of civilizational vitality or of irremediable decay.*

This small nation of approximately 7 million Jewish souls—not much more than the number who were lost in the unthinkable infamy of the Shoah—demonstrates, for all its flaws, the pluck and vigor, the energy, fortitude and tenacity, the essential optimism exemplified in the unapologetic willingness to have children, that seem presently in short supply among Western countries. It is a country whose Diamond Jubilee should be internationally celebrated. It represents a model we should be shooting *for*, not shooting *at*. For in the last analysis, Israel provides an image of the possible while serving as a touchstone of the real.

The grape was pressed from the season's yield
in the vineyard of the time
but the bottles in the rack have been there for millennia
preserved in the cellars of the dark Immemorial.
—Dov Ben-Zamir, *New Wine, Old Bottles*

What Jews cannot be forgiven by their enemies is the rebuilding of a national home. As we have seen, the re-creation of the state of Israel in its phyletic territory is broadly regarded as a colonial incursion into the Middle East and, in many cases, as the latest installment in a vast Jewish conspiracy to pursue the gradual conquest of the world or to assert a sinister hegemony, as proclaimed in the libelous forgery *The Protocols of the Elders of Zion*. This conviction is obviously nonsense if not sheer madness, but it serves a time-dishonored purpose: the justification of an aversion to things Jewish, whether expressed, in Norman Cohn's telling phrase in his book of that title, as a *"warrant for genocide,"* or as a free-floating revulsion to the mere fact of Jewishness—even where no or very few Jews are present.

We find here perhaps the chief grievance of the Western world, or of those who formulate policy and doctrine and those who climb aboard for the ride, against its outrider in the Middle East. Anti-Semitism, or its political manifestation anti-Zionism, must be challenged. The "historical strain of anti-Semitism continues," writes Phyllis Chesler in *The New Anti-Semitism*, "but in the last fifty years it has also metamorphosed into the most violent anti-Zionism." Anti-Zionism, we might say, is merely the kosher form of anti-Semitism.

In effect, the Muslim world and the anti-Semitic left have merely revived the ancient libels. As Raymond Scheindlin documents in *A Short History of the Jewish People*, "Egyptian writers circulated distorted and insulting accounts of Jewish history," claiming that the Jews "originally came to Egypt as alien conquerors, set fire to Egyptian towns, destroyed their temples, and mistreated their inhabitants." As usual, history proves otherwise. These putatively conquering Israelites who were said to have despoiled Egypt in fact constituted a captive population under the Pharaohs.

The Seleucid emperor Antiochus IV Epiphanes, who desecrated the Temple in Jerusalem in 167 BC, was the first historical figure to persecute the Jews for their religion *as such*, and the anti-Semitic virus has been gathering momentum ever since. The Jewish-Roman historian Flavius Josephus tells us in *Against Apion* of a certain 1st century AD grammarian who apparently started the hoary blood libel on its global career. Apion wrote that, "At a set time every year [the Jews] used to catch a Greek foreigner ... and kill him, and sacrifice with their accustomed solemnities, and taste of his entrails." Josephus comments: "Now this is such a most tragical fable as is full of nothing but cruelty and impudence." The "tragical fable" has travelled through the centuries and bred far more than "cruelty and impudence." Isaiah may have been right portraying Israel as a light unto the nations, but a light has at least two properties: it casts a glow, and it can be extinguished.

Robert Spencer points out that, according to an ISIS proclamation and Muslim clerics like Egyptian imam Muhammad Hussein Ya'qoub, the conflict is not about Palestine, not about lands and possessions, but is religious in nature. "If the Jews left Palestine to us," thunders Ya'qoub, "Would we start loving them? Of course not. We will never love them. Absolutely not. The Jews are infidels." Sheikh Said Al-Afani confirmed: "Our hatred of them is purely on religious grounds, and not because of the pure, sacred land ... or because of Gaza." The "Palestine problem" is ancillary to the call for a global jihad against the Jewish people; the campaign against Israel is only the opening salvo in a larger conflict. Israel is considered as the first casualty in a war of extermination. But one way or another, it remains the locus of asylum for the Jewish Diaspora.

It should be said at this juncture that in defending Israel I am not advocating for the classical rabbinical/Lurianic concept of *Tikkun Olam*, the Mishnaic mandate to mend a broken world and reveal the hidden Creator for all mankind to marvel and worship: *Tikkun* means "repair," *Olam*, "for all time." The idea is that the Lord purposely left room for human beings to continuously improve upon His work, a duty imposed upon Jews for the benefit of the human race. It is a lovely theological notion, but it should not come at the expense of exposing one's own people to a bloodthirsty adversary, a decadent commentariat or a hopelessly corrupt United Nations.

A country cannot always be seeking to appease, always deferring victory, always diverting its own resources to benefit others. One recalls that Israel sent a crack rescue team to aid in restoration work after the 2011 tsunami in Japan, a country where many writers, publishers and organizations are preoccupied with *Yudakaya* ("the Jewish peril"). The state-of-the-art medical team and field hospital Israel dispatched to Haiti after the great earthquake of 2010 was venomously maligned among bloggers and journalists as an organ-harvesting operation.

The Israeli Medical Association requires that doctors apply the principle of *comprehensive triage* in battle conditions, even if that means helping terrorists before their victims. Compounding the absurdity, even after withdrawing from Gaza, Israel has continued furnishing an avowed and determined enemy with food, fuel, electricity, medical supplies and building materials. Par for the course, an agreement over offshore natural gas resources saw the former left-wing government cede significant portions of its territorial waters and a gas field to Hezbollah, gaining nothing in return. It seems the moral calculus among Israeli benefactors is self-destructively skewed.

This is *Tikkun Olam* with a vengeance. As Zionist leader Ze'ev Jabotinsky wrote sarcastically, "If you want to be 'good,' allow yourself to be killed and forego all that you made it your aim to defend: home, country, freedom, hope." It shouldn't be this way. "The prophets carried God's message to the Jewish people," explains Jonathan Neumann in *To Heal the World?: How the Jewish Left Corrupts Judaism and Endangers Israel*, "to mend their ways, not the world, and He will do the rest." It is high time that Israel—its political and legal authorities, its commanders, the media and the intellectual elect—adopt a new mode of thinking, symbolized by its Diamond Jubilee.

Israel must get its act together and continue to be, as it has since its founding, a model *by example*, an archetype or paradigm of what is possible in the midst of hostility, revilement and belligerence, namely, the strength to defend one's people and heritage, the clear-headedness to husband one's resources, and the ability to survive and flourish. In his important book *United in Hate: The Left's Romance with Tyranny and Terror*, *FrontPage Magazine* editor Jamie Glazov states that, "Two of the most outstanding Jewish characteristics are the love of life and the enduring struggle to survive." The old Jewish joke is apt: They tried to kill us, we survived, let's eat. The tragic is rendered both comic and stoic. The joke is expressive of a people's fortitude.

> *Abscess makes the heart grow fonder.*
> —Groucho Marx, *The Cocoanuts*

"What is it about the kind of jokes Jews tell," asks Joseph Epstein in The Ideal of Culture, "that is notably, ineluctably Jewish?" Good question. Is it a way of negotiating what Henry James, in an 1896 letter to his friend A. C. Benson, called "the imagination of disaster"? Jewish humor is both a survival technique and a cultural semiotic. It is, writes Ruth Wisse in No Joke, "One of many possible responses to the anomalous experience of the Jews." Even the super-earnest Isaiah's use of the word basar (*Isaiah* 40:8-9), often translated as "preach," carries the nuance of cheerfulness and glad tidings. Abraham's haggling with God has all the marks of an incipient comedy sketch, even if the capper went off-script.

The Israeli-inspired Comedy Central TV cartoon show, *Drawn Together*, highlighting characters with names like Jew Producer, Foxxy Love, Toot Braunstein, Wooldoor Sockbat and Strawberry Shortcake, and making astringent fun for didactic purposes of some of the major currents and events of Jewish history with all its suffering and turmoil, is an expression of both indomitable festivity and wry humility. "I do not know whether there are many other instances," wrote Freud in *Jokes and Their Relation to the Unconscious*, "of a people making fun to such a degree of its own character."

The Jewish Joke is a special case, a way of remaining

solvent in a bear market. Like Noah, the Jew floats his stock in a situation in which everyone else would be in liquidation. Israel's Diamond Jubilee is, in its way, a joke upon the world, albeit a good-humored one. But the issue is always critical. Things can always get worse. As comedian George Burns remarked, "When I was a boy, the Dead Sea was only sick."

One thinks, too, of the Israeli paratrooper joke. "If the chute doesn't open," the newly enrolled paratrooper asks his training officer, "how long until I hit the ground?" The officer answers, "The rest of your life." Regarding the historical friction between Judaism and Christianity, there is a deep understanding in Judaism that Jesus was also a member of "the Tribe" and should be embraced, not rejected. There are four things, the joke goes, that reveal that Jesus was a *gantzer* Jew: he lived at home till he was thirty; he went into his Father's business; he thought his mother was a virgin; and his mother treated him like God.

Perhaps the most scarifying of Jewish jokes, retold by Wisse, distinguishes between two kinds of German Jews, the pessimists who went to Palestine, the optimists who went to Auschwitz—indicating that Jewish life is always perilous, even in Israel. Iran and Saudi Arabia just agreed to re-establish diplomatic ties, which bodes serious trouble for Israel, especially as Iran is reportedly fast approaching the nuclear weapons threshold. In the light of Israel's oft-disputed recognition and its precarious position in the world, *every anniversary day for Israel is today.*

One can only agree with McGill University history professor Gil Troy who wrote for the *Jerusalem Post* that the Jubilee should "culminate in a big, brassy, schmaltzy celebration of Israel ... At this critical moment, we must go big picture, transcending the complexities of the moment to showcase this great story of a broken, wandering, persecuted people finding their way by finding their way home." The Jubilee can be said to resemble the traditional *Purim Spiel*—joyful antics commemorating the survival of the Jews related in the *Book of Esther*, bringing merriment into a somber and violent world.

The day fittingly concludes with an official celebration on Mount Herzl in Jerusalem. Music, parades and formal speeches precede the lighting of 12 torches symbolizing the Twelve Tribes of Israel, of whom only the descendants of the tribes of Judah and Benjamin have survived following their return to the homeland from the Babylonian exile in 586 BC. It is as if the prophecy of Jeremiah had been fulfilled: "The Lord saith I will gather the remnant of my flock out of all the countries whither I have driven them, and will bring them again to their folds, and they shall be fruitful and increase" (*Jeremiah* 23:1-3).

Speaking metaphorically, Israel has crossed the Jordan from its fraught and tumultuous founding on May 14, 1948 to its present existence among the nations of the world, as *mutatis mutandis* its ancestors did on the tenth of the month of Nisan in 1406 BC into the "promised land" of Canaan, and as the Israelites before them crossed the Red Sea harrowed by the Pharaoh's chariots to eventually establish their homeland.

One thinks of Isaiah's prophecy: "The Lord will have mercy on Jacob, and will yet choose Israel, and set them in their own land: and the strangers shall be joined with them, and they shall cleave to the house of Jacob" (*Isaiah* 14:1). The West, for its part, should be crossing the political Jordan to settle in its birthright with its historical forefathers, to be "joined with them," and to gather around the festive table to celebrate modern Israel's 75th birthday. For, like it or not, Israel is both the precursor and the conscience of the West. It is spirit in place.

2

THE PARADOX OF
THE JEWISH MIND

Growing up Jewish in a small Quebec town at a time when an ultramontane clergy dominated social and religious life, I experienced my share of antisemitic hatred. Restricted from visiting certain beaches and playgrounds, regularly ambushed on the way to school by kids screaming anti-Jewish taunts and slurs (the obscenity of choice was *maudit juif,* "damned Jew"), arrested once for defending myself against a gang of thugs, thus contributing, no doubt, to what is known as the "cycle of violence"—to mention only a few such incidents—I learned at first-hand what it means to be a Jew. Obviously, it was not like trying to survive in Lithuania or Germany, but it was a revelation nonetheless.

I recall one episode in which I was not personally involved but which was the most vividly instructive of all. Several times a year, professional wrestlers from Montreal would visit the village sports center and regale us with flying jets of sweat, bellows, grunts and body slams. On one such occasion, a masked behemoth was pitted against a lesser opponent wearing blue and white trunks embellished with the Star of David. It didn't take long before this substitute Jew was brutally demolished to the cheers and hoots of an appreciative crowd. The *coup de grâce* came when the methodical tormenter, after having thoroughly administered a vicious beating, scooped up a handful of sawdust from the floor of the arena and rubbed it into his victim's eyes. The blinded "Jew" staggered about the ring, arms flailing, crying out to the Jewish god—*Aidez-moi*, Seigneur, "Help me, Lord." After a minute or so of histrionic misery, he was clutched by the hair, driven head first into the ring post, and then hurled through the ropes unto the ground several feet below. A team of assistants appeared and carried him out on a stretcher, surrounded by a gesticulating mob.

It all seemed real then and I was young enough to be horrified by what I had just witnessed. It was only much later that I recognized this staged event as the symbolic equivalent of a blinded people mauled and battered into a state of insensibility. Worse, I began to wonder whether a people finding itself in the ring of near-universal opprobrium, or at least a significant proportion of them, were not busily engaged rubbing sand into their own eyes. And I am no less horrified now than I was as a young spectator at a fake wrestling match.

Israel has made a major breakthrough in radiation monitoring technology. The Environmental Protection Ministry announced that it will be deploying a new detection system that will enable continuous real-time monitoring of radiation hazards from cellular antennas, establishing the country as a world leader in the field. A similar device to detect the harmful radiation from bad ideas that damage the capacity of Jews and Israelis to resist ideological contamination would be even more welcome. Perhaps the requisite apparatus is already in place, only not fully activated. It's called "the mind."

Israel is a threatened nation, not only because it is surrounded by enemies who would like nothing better than to drive its people into the sea, but because it is increasingly regarded and treated in the international arena as a pariah state, vilified in the media, subject to boycotts, falsely condemned as an apartheid regime, its officials tarred as war criminals. We know the drill now: first comes the pummeling, then the expulsion from the ring. One recalls the rantings of former presidential advisor Zbigniew Brzezinski or the blatant fabrications of professor John Mearsheimer, co-author of *The Israel Lobby*, among innumerable other influential and surreptitious antisemites, if there is any doubt about the intention to delegitimize Israel—and Jews.

As for the Jewish community in the Diaspora, it too confronts a swelling and malignant antisemitism even in countries where Jew-hatred has been in approximate re-mission. This is why of all ethnic groups, it is the least able to tolerate—I must be blunt—the number of un-reconstructed idiots, useful or otherwise, proliferating in its midst, whether they are prone to delusions of nobil-ity and grandeur or merely self-interested schemers for whom, to cite *Deuteronomy* 16:19, "a gift [i.e., bribe] doth blind the eyes of the wise, and pervert the words of the righteous." They are equally at risk, both those who turn toward the ineffable and lofty in the realm of ideas and those who turn basely against their own. And their num-ber, I'm afraid, is legion.

Leaving aside for now the vast constituency of or-dinary Jews who vote for the Liberal Party in Canada and the Democrats in the U.S., for which the welfare of the Jewish state, to put it mildly, is not on the agenda, or left-wing Israelis devoted to the mirage of surrendering land for "peace," let us take a very brief sampling of high-pro-file figures who have been in the news over the last decade or so.

There is jurist Richard Goldstone who fathered the heinous U.N. report largely blaming Israel for its conduct during Operation Cast Lead—the same man who accept-ed a judicial appointment during the apartheid era in south Africa and who, according to reports, was responsible for sending 28 blacks to their death; political careerist Martin Indyk, harshly critical of the beleaguered Jewish state he apparently once supported; academic maven Neve Gordon who denounces his home country, sides with the Palestinians and offered comfort to Yassir Arafat in the Mukataa compound during the Intifada; visual artist Jan Egesborg circulating maps with Israel blanked out and featuring the phrase "Final Solution;" journalist Uri Blau of *Haaretz* newspaper in illegal possession of sensitive state documents; Nobelized scientist Ada Yonath who urges the Israeli government to release its terrorist prisoners; literary cynosure David Grossman whose slogan, "peace of no choice," would, if taken seriously, ultimately deprive him of it; ersatz intellectual Naomi Klein who considers Israel a terror state; Hannah Rosenthal, former director of the U.S. Office to Monitor and Combat Anti-Semitism, who has neither monitored nor combated it, but generally let it pass under the radar; revisionist Tom Segev faulting the Jewish state for being over-hasty and paranoid; activist Naomi Chazan, former president of the New Israel Fund which sponsors left-wing, anti-Israel NGOs; the late historian Tony Judt who would dissolve Israel into an Arab-majority "binational" state; orchestra conductor and pianist Daniel Barenboim, friend to the late anti-Israeli ideologue Edward Said; aptly-named author Shlomo Sand, who in his *The Invention of the Jewish People* attempts to deprive Jews of their historic and biblical identity, despite the genetic markers which decisively refute his thesis; Rabbi Michael Lerner, publisher of

Tikkun Magazine and a self-proclaimed "spiritual progressive," who accuses Israel of wantonly maiming and killing Palestinians; Israel's *soi-disant* "top philosopher" Avishai Margolit, who advocates a return to the porous and indefensible 1948 borders which he calls "little Israel," though a better designation might then be "no Israel at all;" and progressivist historian Howard Zinn for whom Israel is a "mistake."

This, as I indicate, is only the merest cross-section of a teeming multitude of familiar names that could fill an *Almanach de Gotha* of the gullible, the obtuse or the treacherous. They are all what we would regard as "intelligent" people, but their intelligence is specific to their fields and does not correlate especially well with what I will call the *gi* factor (on the model of the psychometrical category *g*, mental ability), that is, general intelligence, founded in common sense, which is able to transcend the boundaries and constraints of specific disciplines.

Of all the peoples of the world, Jews can least afford to be stupid, or merely *selectively* brilliant. What is the point of excelling at chemistry, or jurisprudence, or music, or philosophy, or literature, or medicine or any other subject—Jews represent 0.2 percent of world population but 22.4 percent of Nobel laureates—if there is not much *gi* behind it, if the Jewish mind is incapable of coming to grips with a complex, unforgiving, belligerent and *actual* world that has never fully accepted the Jew as a fellow human being and has often moved to humiliate, oppress and, indeed, exterminate him. Such smart-stupid Jews are the affliction of their people and, in the last analysis, their own worst enemies. For in the event of another antisemitic rampage or genocide—which by their indifference, complicity or quixotic utopianism they would have helped to bring about—they too, just like their targeted ancestors and regardless of their achievements, would be flung into the ditches of history.

Israel, we know, is on the cutting edge of brain science, providing key elements in terms of staff, resources and infrastructure for the ongoing Blue Brain Project. The Jerusalem center for neural computation is the most advanced such institute in the world. Speaking metaphorically, it is rather ironic that discoveries in the field of neurocomputation do not necessarily carry over into daily practice, down-to-earth reasonableness and, let's say, survival acumen. For many Jews, what fills the space where gi should be are dreams, visions and tractionless speculations, grand schemes for a better world, and an ethereal sense of ideal justice oblivious to the corrugations of reality. This for the most part is what constitutes the "Jewish sensibility:" local proficiency wedded to utopian exhalations—if not, that is, exploiting anti-Zionism for profit and advantage.

We might say that the distinction between general intelligence and specific intelligence is like that between honey and sugar. What the bees do is different from what the beets do. General intelligence is undifferentiatedly curious, wide-ranging and panoramic; specific intelligence is specialized, rooted in particulars and fixed inside a bounded expertise, no matter how flexible its perimeters. We Jews, it seems, are good at *si* but there is far too little *gi* among us, and we will pay in suffering for this deficit unless we eventually learn to think outside the boxcar.

I write this as a Jew who is utterly mortified by the self-injurious imbecility I see escalating throughout the community to which I presumably belong. The propagation of foolish ideas, lunatic affiliations and galloping myopia among an otherwise accomplished people has left me not only bewildered but also, it pains me to confess, resentful. With too few exceptions, the "peaceniks" march toward a calamity of their own devising; Jewish organizations naively succumb to the "charm offensives" of their deceptive adversaries; and the "intellectuals," true to their class, are intoxicated with earnest inanities and clever-sounding verbiage. This is especially true of many Israeli academics in the forefront of "Israel Apartheid Week," hate fests that, in the words of former chair of Hillel UK Brenda Katten, "educate toward the demise of Israel." Jews have to be smarter than that. For Jews do not enjoy the luxury of historical illiteracy or the tainted privilege of self-denial. They cannot, like Peter Schlemiel, lose their shadow, no matter how hard they work at it—

as if one could indemnify oneself against oneself, as if, to quote Horace Kallen, one could change one's grandfather. Ehrich Weisz, aka Harry Houdini, was a Jewish escape artist but even he, the Master, was taken off guard and could not evade the bitter dereliction that lay in store for him.

Let us make no mistake about this, the darkness is rising again. The "culture of hatred" that Robert Wistrich minutely anatomizes in *A Lethal Obsession*, a phenomenon, as he writes, "that has over centuries produced an almost unfathomable abyss of dehumanization of the Jews," is growing increasingly pervasive in the modern world. What, then, can one say to a lineage of self-defectors and sand-eyed agonists, these Jewish dream merchants on the one hand and *machers* on the other, these airy Margolits or squalid Goldstones trading respectively in the coin of delirium or betrayal?

Perhaps just one thing. Time to wake up and smell the cordite.

3

GEORGE JONAS AND BEETHOVEN'S MASK

In the Preface to his memoirs, *Beethoven's Mask: Notes on My Life and Times*, novelist and political columnist George Jonas quotes his wit-dispensing and oracular father, a professional baritone reminiscing about his role in Verdi's *Un Ballo In Maschera*. The world reminded Jonas-*père* of a masked ball. Europe in particular was a Venetian carnival, with assassins dressed up as lyric poets. Political butchers lurked in ducal palaces, wearing Beethoven's mask, so to speak, to showcase the power and wealth of the nobility. Beethoven' mask could be construed as a symbol of Europe's highest achievements in creative vitality hiding the cruel reality of corruption and exploitation. Along with its man-

ifest glories, European civilization was an abattoir with the imposing façade of an opera house in which masked figures strutted and promenaded, plying the recitative of violence and coercion.

Waiting in the wings of this feral and ludicrous—but also fascinating—performance is the newest member of the cast, a muezzin with a loudspeaker, calling suicide bombers to prayer. So begins *Beethoven's Mask*. The author steps forward as protagonist in a kind of modern masque or mixed opera with its multiple plot lines, intricate figurations, and, as is often the case, menacing backdrop, finding as he sets it all down that the story is absurd and troubling, but the music compelling.

Jonas is not averse to the idea of the mask *per se*, and indeed comes equipped with his own elaborate panoply of expository guises: adventurer, lover, philosopher, political analyst, poet, prodigal son, wandering Jew, lay theologian, everyday Beethoven, librettist par excellence. As he warms to his subject, Jonas introduces us to his high-school music teacher in postwar Budapest, with the cumbrous nickname of Chief Cow and the forbidding features of a Beethoven death mask. Among the pedagogue's various obligations was the practical duty of distributing milk to his students, which accounted for his sobriquet. This, too, is one of the masks Jonas wears—the mask of the preceptor who nourishes us with a lifetime's learning and tested wisdom.

But there is one mask that Jonas adamantly refuses to wear, the dubious mask of justice, behind which political fashions and ideological agendas regularly hide. There will be no dissembling here. Instead, Jonas puts on an entertaining but wholly candid performance, switching from one key to another, oscillating between the poles of the *vita activa* and the *vita contemplativa*, inditing arias, reciting poems, cracking jokes, telling stories, but also offering an acid critique of contemporary mores and a reminder that, in the last analysis, we do not live in a simulacrum or an allegory. The murders that take place on the world's stage, lurid or flamboyant, leave real corpses behind.

The structuring metaphor is a complex one and cuts in several directions, since the mask may function as both a deception and a disclosure, a form of camouflage and the presumable expression of character. Or perhaps it is not simply a question of one or the other but of the dialectical interplay between mask and face, with Jonas and, by implication, the larger culture, resembling the phantom of the opera (Gaston Leroux, author of *Le Fantôme de l'opéra*, is mentioned in text), with only half-mask cloaking partial disfigurement and making lush Weberian music to carry the improbable plot.

Whatever way we parse these involutions, the issue here is really one of identity—of the unstable amalgam of good and evil, humor and portentousness, probity and folly, labored truth and facile delusion, rooted ancestry and windborne autonomy, the authentic and the imaginary—that constitutes what we call personality, from the Latin root *persona*, or mask. These are questions that Jonas has deeply considered. In writing his memoirs, he composes his self by trying on, that is, narrating, a series of apt and congenial correlates or masks. In doing so, the essential features of that fugitive modality begin to emerge, those of the picaro-of-letters, antic philosopher, and savvy chronicler of the modern age.

And so, in glittering prose and coruscating wit, he proceeds to construct not only a sprightly autobiography but a sober historical document. The miscellany of personal episodes he regales us with (the Life) are both amusing and poignant: the gallery of memorable relatives, the narrow escapes under the Nazis and the Communists, the ladies, the jobs, the eccentric friends and mentors, the passion for flying and motorcycle racing. But the real substance of the book (the Times) comprises a set of somber reflections on the century we have just survived and the century we may not. Thus, we are given an astute political analysis of the organizing principles around which countries, commonwealths, and supranational entities cohere, with a view to explaining both the collapse of the Soviet Union, the long-term fragility of the European Union and the insecure prospects of Western civilization.

Closer to home, there follows a devastating etiology of the Canadian sickness, the disease of "third wave statism," which could accomplish precisely what Fascism and Communism failed to achieve. In Jonas's estimation, Canada, with its Ottawa-dominated central planning, social engineering, and effectively command economy, is the glossiest, the most sophisticated, and the most up-to-date version of the illiberal state, modern Europe's transatlantic outpost. His description of the fine Canadian art of fence-sitting is equally trenchant. Since the 1960s Canada has tried to achieve moral leadership by observing strict neutrality between good and evil. And his put-down of the CBC, where he spent much of his salaried life (and this writer spent three years of his), should be read by anyone who still believes in the competence, relevance, and impartiality of the national broadcaster.

Jonas subsequently turns his attention to what has been called "the Jewish question," which is central to his understanding of self and thus occupies a major portion of the text. For a Jew who, until his marriage to Barbara Amiel in 1974, had never seen the inside of a synagogue, the issues of Jewish continuity and identity have come to acquire a belated importance. Jonas acknowledges that his Jewish wedding may have corresponded with "something felt, deeply if dimly, in my otherwise secular being," but concludes, "I ponder these contradictions...this too is Jewish continuity, I suppose." His construal of the malignant phenomenon of anti-Semitism and the puzzle of Jewish identity is also worth reading as yet another contribution to the literary and diagnostic attempt to shed light on such tortuous dilemmas.

These passages are reminiscent of earlier self-questioning in the work of Jewish thinkers like Peter Gay, Hans Mayer (aka Jean Améry), Alain Finkielkraut, and Eric Hobsbawm. In *Weimar Culture*, for example, Gay writes that some Germans ... discovered themselves to be Jews because the Nazi government told them that is what they were. Mayer, in *At The Mind's Limits*, recounts that he found out he was a Jew with the passing of the Nuremburg Laws in 1935. Finkielkraut, reflecting on his experience in France, entitles one of his books *Le juif imaginaire*, and Hobsbawm, about as non-Jewish a Jew as one can hope to find, comments in his memoir, *Interesting Times*, "though entirely unobservant, we nevertheless knew that we were, and could not get away from, being Jews."

Similarly, Jonas writes that his Jewishness was not defined by dietary laws, Friday candles, or Hebrew phrases in a prayer book. It was defined by "a yellow star sewn to my lapel by my mother, in my native Budapest, as required by Nazi law." The question becomes: Is the inside, so to speak, determined by the outside? Is the kaleidoscope shaken by an external hand to create a pattern or the semblance of a pattern, so that an identity is projected upon the Jew by a world for which the many conflicting aspects of Judaism, its multiplicity of competing practices and convictions, and the perplexity of the individual postulant are of no account whatsoever? As the father of Zionism, Theodor Herzl, wrote in his founding pamphlet, *The Jewish State*, "the Jews were one people—our enemies have made us one."

The issue of external reification notwithstanding, the mystery of Jewish identity and self-definition persists. In seeking a solution to this conundrum, Jonas dismisses, perhaps a little too casually, the factors of nation, faith, and cultural derivation, which leaves only tribal affiliation, coupled with a cultural choice. You were a Jew precisely if you were of Jewish descent, and continued to define yourself as Jewish. The notion of Jewish descent, however, merely begs the question, since it does not specify what actually does the descending—the rabbinical orders, the prophetic heritage, the competing sects and schisms, the rules of observance often honored in the breach?

For its part, the idea of choice, of self-election, may, perhaps, serve as a partial though significant determinant. The elusiveness of a metaphysical identity-core does not preclude the possibility of acceding to a historical option, of voluntary self-identification as a Jew in one's own as well as the world's eyes. Freud himself, in the Preface to the Hebrew translation of *Totem and Taboo*, claimed that he grasped his own Jewishness in its very essence, although he could not now express that essence clearly in words. The Jew remains a Jew—I believe Jonas would concur—because he cannot validly discard nearly 80 generations of quasi-nucleic substance that creates a feeling of collective belonging, even if he cannot say with assurance precisely what he belongs to, and because at some level he intuits that the world will not tolerate indefinitely the ruses of self-evasion or the assumption of secularity he is tempted to embrace.

Perhaps the most critically penetrating aspect of this book is Jonas's prolonged examination of the so-called "New Left." One might regard it as a study of the intellectual malady of being wrong about nearly everything while claiming ideological infallibility and the moral high ground. Jonas does not mince words. This infirmity, he asserts, affects mainly individuals of above-average learning, intellect, and moral preoccupation (or conceit). Certain errors require high IQs. The prevalence of intellectual error also entails a broad community of assent, the approval of those who have been educated beyond their intellectual means and who provide support for the left-liberal ethos that dominates the contemporary sensibility.

It is not always easy to tell whether the rot starts at the top or the bottom, among the intellectual class or, as Jonas puts it, "among illiterates who have been taught to read and write," that social echelon of cultural consumers without culture who suffer from mass curriculitis. Does the top reflect the bottom or is the bottom contaminated from above? Clearly, the top bears a greater responsibility for the spread of the syndrome, in virtue of its didactic authority, its access to research materials, its enjoyment of privileged time for scholarship, and ultimately, its capacity to produce via the media what counts as a profane Vulgate.

Jonas freely admits that his political allegiance is a neoconservative one, but observes that the currently pejorative term "neoconservative" is really a misapplied synonym for classical liberal. As such, Jonas does not scruple to indict the Left for a veritable blizzard of fallacies and misconceptions, including its protracted love affair with the Soviet Union; its embrace of the Arab states which were Moscow's political clients; its adopting the cause of the Palestinian resistance, which (as he writes in *Vengeance*) had itself resolved by the late 1960s to make common cause with international Communism; its rejection of Israel, which it sees as a colonial beachhead of the United States; its retention of Marxist principles even after the collapse of the Soviet empire and the evident bankruptcy of Communism as a worldwide salvific movement; its inability or unwillingness to confront the theocratic and totalitarian forces abroad in the world—and, indeed, to incorporate them; and its craven tendency to call a spade a spud, huddling behind the language of political correctness that prevents the West from identifying the enemy who schemes its destruction and the real nature of events impinging upon it with ever-increasing ferocity. For Jonas, the ideology that now governs the academy, the trade unions, the media, and our political elites, with their mark-down ideas and baleful influence on public opinion, may well be the most insidious threat we face.

At the conclusion of these memoirs, resembling at one and the same time classical masque, beggar's op-era, and tragic oratorio, Beethoven's mask reappears as a framed drawing on his wall, a death mask of the compos-er sketched by the author's mother as an art class assign-ment, and dated 9/11, 1920. The date is, of course, eerily premonitory, heralding not the end of history, as some have claimed, but the end of history as most of us have known it. The death mask hanging on the wall bears the lineaments of a great civilization in all its operatic magni-tude that now seems effectively moribund, witlessly col-luding with its own demise. The music composed by Bee-thoven is conducted by Clio, the Muse of History, who has another grand finale in mind. The kettledrums can still be heard, but the notes of a classical harmony have been drawn and quartered.

Beethoven's Mask is in many ways an extraordinary performance, rich in pageantry and orchestration, its tim-bre gradually deepening as it approaches its denouement. For what begins as a collection of reminiscences, obiter dicta, anecdotes, cultural analytics, and assorted commen-taries on this and that ends up sounding very much like a requiem for a civilization. It recalls Beethoven's opera

Fidelio, which contains great and resonating music, the Leonore #3 overture, the memorable Prisoners Chorus, and repeated trumpet calls from offstage, mingled with a considerable amount of *Singspiel*, proliferating subplots, disguises, and comic flourishes. The mode is distinctly playful, at least initially, but there is a solemn turn toward the introduction of serious and weighty musical themes, so that a certain inconsistency of tone seems to permeate the score. And yet, as in *Fidelio*, we know that in *Beethoven's Mask*, with all its tonal and thematic syncopations, we are in the presence of a complex and substantial work which will continue to reverberate on a far larger stage than the personal.

4

THE IDEAL OF PERFECTION IN FAITH AND POLITICS

The quest for the ideal is a human predisposition that shapes every social movement, political program and religious communion. As we survey a world mired in war and social upheaval, we note seminal and competing conceptions of the ideal in human affairs. The socialist ideal of human perfectibility has failed everywhere it has been tried, and is currently failing wherever we look. The Islamic ideal of a humanity acceptable to Allah has resulted in oceans of bloodshed, insoluble antagonisms and political dysfunction on a global scale. The Judeo-Christian ideal in its various forms, religious and secular, while quixotic in its progress and subject to sanguinary lapses, has enjoyed comparative success in providing for human happiness and prosperity.

Is there a single factor that distinguishes the philosophies that enable human flourishing from those that inevitably produce mass misery and political disarray? To

simplify in the interests of clarity, we can say that acceptance of human limitation is key to the avoidance of totalitarianism. A consideration of the ideals that underlie
Socialism and Islam, in comparison with the Jewish and
Christian worldviews, as well as Western classical Liberalism, which today goes by the name of Conservatism, may
serve to make the case.

In Judaism, the ideal of perfection falls beyond the
grasp of fallible man. The Jewish ideal is not so much
represented as *intimated* by a series of commandments
that are mainly negative in character, as if to recognize
the impetuous tendency to transgression and the limits of
human perfectibility. The ideal is embodied not in particular individuals (many of whom are deeply flawed) but diffused through a veritable cast of characters—patriarchs
(Abraham, Isaac, Jacob), prophets (Elijah, Jeremiah, Isaiah), and leaders (Moses, Joshua, David). Further, unlike
the principal faiths and collectivist movements, Judaism
does not seek to proselytize but to witness and survive.

For Christians, the ideal of perfection exists in Heav-
en and is incarnated in Jesus, whose example can be ap-
proximated but never literally incorporated. The *imitatio
Christi* can be practiced but never fully consummated. It is
nonetheless a remedial and, in its core presuppositions, a
temperate discipline. As St. Augustine taught, the City of
God and the City of Man are two distinct entities. Thomas
à Kempis in *The Imitation of Christ* preached a retreat from

the world into contemplation, and Saint Francis of Assisi devoted himself to poverty and good works, as recorded in The Little Flowers of Saint Francis. In this sense, humility—though not always in evidence—is inherent in the Christian *approach* to an ideal fulfillment. Furthermore, the idea of conquest and forcible constraint has been refined out of historical Christianity in the way it has never been banished, for example, from Islamic doctrine and usage.

Conservative political thought comes in many different shades but shares with Judaism and Christianity a default position regarding the application of the ideal in customary practice. In other words, what it regards as an ideal— "piecemeal social engineering" in Karl Popper's now-misconceived phrase from The Open Society and Its Enemies, or trial-and-error gradualism in improving society—cannot by definition be imposed by force. Freedom of debate and assembly, equality before the law, and a democratic franchise based on popular representation are functions of an ideal that exists in the moral and political imagination, that is carried by frail and errant human beings, and that is always in process.

On the other hand, for communism and socialism, the ideal exists in the future and its material facsimile, their adherents believe, can eventually be wrested through violence and/or radical forms of legislation into an imminent present. In effect, Communism and its variants are predicated on the assumption that human nature can be modified, trained and ultimately transformed; that is, it is based on a fantasy that cannot come to terms with the unbridgeable gap between the ideal and the real. Leftist politics valorizes an ideal—equality of outcome regardless of input, redistribution of wealth, levelling of social and personal distinctions, communal ownership of resources, infallible guidance of a managerial elite—that does not exist in the realm of human possibility, and the attempt to realize and impose it is always doomed to failure and the unleashing of monstrous perversions.

For Islam, by contrast, the ideal of human behavior and political organization is understood already to exist in the world—it is Islam itself. It too must be imposed, leading equally with the Communist-Socialist axis to macabre deformations of social and political life. But the distinctions are critical. The Islamic ideal—which no longer abides *exclusively* in the sphere of the divine, nor in a partly unattainable skein of rules and proscriptions, nor in the halting process of beneficial social development, nor in a future to be born by C-section—came into the world, actually and concretely, with Muhammad, the "perfect man," whom every genuine Muslim must seek to emulate, theoretically, *to become*. The Salafist return to origins in its quest to revive a pristine communion and consolidate it in the present is not merely a puritanical variant of Islam, as Muslim revisionists propose, but the very crux of Islamic perfectionism. The blueprint for the perfect life as it existed in the past needs only to be recognized. It is in some way already here and perennially achievable, needing only to be disclosed and ready to be followed at any time.

The bedrock ideals of Socialism and Islam are distorted and indeed grotesque programs for human development. The Leftist mentality is intrinsically self-contradictory. "Man is born free," claimed Rousseau, the father of modern Socialism and Marx's precursor, "and everywhere he is in chains" —raising the insoluble paradox of how it is that men born free set about forging chains in which to imprison their fellows as well as themselves. The entire project sinks into nonsense at its very origins and can be established only by deception and violence. As the saying beloved by communists and socialists goes (coined by a French royalist, *Vendée* leader François de Charette), you have to break eggs to make an omelette. The trouble is, the eggshells that shard the omelette render it inedible. As Milovan Djilas noted in *The Unperfect Society*, the end does not justify the means when the means violate the purpose of the end.

In the present era Islam represents an immediate menace to our way of life as the West finds itself increasingly under the blade of the Islamic scimitar, from the "lone wolf" machete to the Iranian "arc of fire." There is no doubt that we have a serious and perhaps intractable problem with Islam, and anyone who denies it is living in a fool's paradise. As Winston Churchill wrote in *The River*

War, the dilemma we confront is that Islam represents a "retrograde force" in the world, appealing to those darker aspects of human nature which Western jurisprudence, political thought and liberal values have tended, albeit with varying success, to amend and reform.

Socialism lives in the present-future and Islam in the present-past. Enlightened Western thought, grounded in Judeo-Christian civilization, lives in neither. It recognizes that man is a morally defective and politically flawed creature, for whom progress moves by fits and starts and is always subject to limitations of character and possibility. The classic Western ideal is asymptotic, always in flux, constitutively elusive, never completely realizable, in order to prevent tyrannical asphyxia and cultural ossification, as well as the insufferable conceit of self-declared benefactors. It is never fixed or dispositive, as in the Socialist and Islamic conceptions of human betterment. We might say that it is in the present *but not of it*, constantly moving toward another, better present *at which it will never arrive*. In other words, the past is to be remembered but not reproduced, while the future is not an ultimately realizable end-point—the glaring error of lapsed conservative Francis Fukayama in *The End of History and the Last Man*. The temporal dimension in which the Judeo-Christian ideal resides is a succession of ever-changing presents, knowing that an eschatological terminal is not within the human ken.

The cadastral address of the Socialist ideal, as we've noted, is located in the indefinite future, but it squats in the here and now so that it seems substantial and refuses to be evicted. It merely creates tenement states, renting time until the day history is abolished and the devil's pleasure palace, in Michael Walsh's titular phrase, is erected *in perpetuum*. The Islamic ideal resides permanently among us, fully formed, repressive and immutable, working in tandem with aspects of the Socialist model. Indeed, Socialism prepares the way for Islam, as in Sweden, Norway, France, the U.K., and increasingly in Germany and Canada—before Islam in any of its national expressions is strong enough to turn and destroy the Left root and branch, as happened in Iran after Ayatollah Khomeini's successful revolution. For, once dominant, Islam is by nature unable to coexist with any other social, political or religious organization.

The Socialist agenda and the Islamic world-view, forms of topiary art applied to human beings, represent similar ideals of both minute and overarching social control which cannot be disarmed or interpreted out of existence. They must be resisted with every means at our disposal. If we continue to misconceive such totalitarian systems, whose *present manifestations* are respectively oriented toward a reified future and a reified past, they will inevitably undermine the *proximate* ideals of the essential Judeo-Christian West and its vulnerable Conservative heritage. The core Judeo-Christian principle of humility and uncertainty in facing both the divine and the future is now under greater threat than ever.

5

THE JEWISH
INTELLECTUAL
PREDICAMENT

I broach once again, as I have several times before, the curious phenomenon of Jewish intelligence, so competent across the disciplines and professions, yet so feckless and inept when it comes to taking stock of its precarious position in the world and working to ensure its own perpetuation. I've suggested a heuristic distinction between specialized intelligence and general intelligence, with Jews excelling at the former and often lamentably deficient in the latter. Jewish accomplishments in music, mathematics, literature, theology, economics, science and jurisprudence are legendary. At the same time, millennia of social and cultural quarantine must have their effect on the sensibility of a people, producing a being who is always in danger of contracting that wasting disease which Ruth Wisse in *Jews and Power* has diagnosed as "the veneration of political weakness" —not a smart move given the bloody historical register.

There is also a powerful strain of self-loathing and self-betrayal in the Jewish sensibility, exemplified by the personage whom Wisse anatomizes as "the ubiquitous informer, or *moser* … For every Mordecai and Esther who risked their lives to protect fellow Jews, there were schemers who turned betrayal or conversion to profit." This is as true today as it was yesterday and the day before that, and as it is likely to be tomorrow, assuming there is one. We can plot the long chronicle of perfidy along a continuum from the iconic to the picayune, let us say from Cain who slew his own brother to Josh Levinger, an MIT lab technician and member of the anti-Israel International Solidarity Movement, who invented the "Boycott Toolkit." This is described in a press announcement as "a resource where users can generate lists of specific products and companies targeted for boycotts [and] locations of stores that sell each product." To paraphrase Lee Kaplan of *Stop the ISM* website, who has written about this latest development, in today's high-tech environment there's even an app for treachery against Jews. *And it was provided by a Jew.* This is only another way in the spectrum between violence and abject treachery of refusing to be one's brother's keeper, what Yoram Hazony in *The Jewish State: The Struggle for Israel's Soul* calls "a carnival of self-loathing." Edward Alexander's *Jews Against Themselves* is the definitive text in exploring this perilous Jewish tropism and repays frequent consultation.

Being Jewish, I have tried, intently if not quite successfully, to understand this mysterious and self-destructive tendency that prospers in the Jewish soul. Being Canadian, I have been appalled, to take a recent example, at the ignorance on display by the *Centre for Israel and Jewish Affairs*, which condemned the visit of Christine Anderson, who represents the *Alternative for Germany* (AfD) in the European Parliament and whom the Centre described as a member of a party "known for Islamophobic and anti-immigrant views." This is abject nonsense. Anderson is a realist and a brave campaigner for truth. She believes, for example, that the COVID vaccines were experimental and has opposed unfettered Muslim immigration into Germany and Europe—two destructive policies threatening Europe's cohesion. She also famously denounced Canada's authoritarian, Communist China-loving prime minister Justin Trudeau as "a disgrace." How could any sane and responsible Jewish group object to her presence among us?

It should be immediately evident to anyone who thinks about it that such indifference to the sanguinary lessons of history—whether out of a benign identification with the supposedly universal aspirations of mankind, known in Hebrew as the *yetzer hatov*, or the malign inclination toward defection from principle and unscrupulous opportunism, the *yetzer hara*—must inevitably lead to self-immolation. For that matter, to these traditional

Hebrew terms we might propose a third, the *yetzer ba'arout*, or the inclination to ignorance, which is equally noxious and no less widespread. All three *yetzerim* invite disaster. In the last analysis, the antisemite does not distinguish between Jews; even those he regards as accomplices would not be spared in a final reckoning.

There is a passage in Amos Oz's *A Tale of Love and Darkness* which makes this running together of distinctions painfully clear. Referring to the Nazi cleansing operations in the Polish town of Rovno, he writes: "the Germans opened fire and slaughtered on the edge of pits, in two days, some twenty-five thousand souls ... well-to-do and proletarian, pious, assimilated, and baptized, communal leaders, synagogue functionaries, peddlers and drawers of water, Communists and Zionists, intellectuals, artists, and village idiots, and some four thousand babies." As I commented in *The Big Lie*, "the message is that we're all incriminated. Warm Jews, lukewarm Jews and cold Jews are equally at risk. At the end of the day, the antisemite never stopped to take their temperature."

It matters little which of the three inner dispositions or *yetzerim* governs Jewish thought and behavior, be it the tropism toward the "good" that issues in a kind of unanchored evangelism at the expense of one's own well-being; or the inclination toward communal infidelity, the breaking faith with one's threatened collective for one's own sordid advantage; or just plain ignorance, lethargy and intellectual vagrancy. Removed from the social and political dynamic of what historian Robert Wistrich calls "the longest hatred," *hatov, hara,* and *ba'arout* lean alarmingly toward the same destination.

Psychologist Scot Gardiner in *Roots, Episodes, Cohorts* conceives of good and evil "not as a dichotomy but as a dimension;" those "at the ends of the scale" are still related. The same is true of the *three yetzerim,* the good, the bad and the ugly, which all have the potential to divert attention from the essential issue: *continuation.* In the absence of common sense, grounded in a knowledge of history and a willingness to survey and confront the world *as it is,* in other words, in the absence of non-specific or general intelligence, none of the three catalytic propensities has much survival value.

To begin with, the unreflected practice of the *yetzer hatov* is no guarantee of divine favor and certainly not of earthly longevity. The temptation to embrace the high abstractions of universal justice, ecumenical peace and various lofty idealisms of purpose and belief seems endemic to the ethical component of the Jewish mind. Perhaps generations of Torah study and Talmudic speculation have led inexorably to a passion for remote implausibilities and the esoteric delight in intricate or elevated fantasies. Being lost in thought leads to being lost in the world, specific intelligence and notable accomplishments notwithstanding.

Albert Einstein, to take a resonant example, was by general consent a pretty smart guy and one of the two or three greatest physicists who ever lived. His mind could traverse the mathematical contours of time, gravity and space—his proper discipline—but when it came to Israel and the hard thinking necessary for ensuring its survival in the boiling cauldron of the Middle East, he was a veritable dummy. Much like that dubious glory of the Jewish people Martin Buber, Einstein believed that Israel should strive to entrench a form of cultural Zionism in its communal soil. But he repudiated Zionism as a nationalist enterprise, which required the maintenance of defensible borders and a spirit of martial vigor and self-assertion. Speaking at a seder in New York, as reported in Walter Isaacson's *Einstein: His Life and Universe*, he told his audience that his "awareness of the essential nature of Judaism resists the idea of a Jewish state with borders, an army, and a measure of temporal power." A political innocent, he could not see that absenting such facts and qualities, Israel might never have come into existence or would have been rapidly obliterated once it had.

The same is more or less true of another Jewish luminary, Avishai Margolit, feted as Israel's "foremost philosopher." A founding member of *Peace Now*, which should tell us all we need to know, Margolit insists that Israel should lift the "siege" of Gaza, forgetting that the so-called siege allows thousands of tons of supplies, medicines and electrical power to transit from Israel into Gaza, except when the crossings are closed owing to Hamas sniper fire and mortar bombardments or when the Ashkelon generator comes under attack. The great philosopher also appears untroubled by the prospect of suicide bombers and guerilla fighters sifting into Israel as students, laborers and patients. Further, Margolit does not seem aware of the fact—he has much company here—*that Israel is under no obligation, neither domestic nor international, neither legal nor moral, to victual and replenish an uncompromising enemy.* What other nation on the planet would commit a folly of this nature? Margolit may be an acclaimed "thinker," but he is neither wise nor street-smart. The fatuousness of his proposals is exceeded only by the dangers they would unleash. In short, Margolit is a typical Jewish savant of emeritus caliber, crowned with laurels and showered with awards, dispensing nuggets of pseudo-sagacity, and completely irrelevant.

Then there are the Jews who embody the *yetzer hara*, the propagators of lies and harms. These are Jews like Neve Gordon of Ben-Gurion University, famous for describing the country that pays his salary, which he is apparently in no hurry to forgo, as an "apartheid state," and for having raised his arms in solidarity with Yasser Arafat in his Mukataa compound during the last intifada. Or Bard College professor Joel Kovel who has published a book titled *Overcoming Zionism* in which he condemns the creation of Israel, places the term Islamo-Fascism in scare quotes, traffics in barefaced lies ("Israel's bombing of ambulances," its deliberate targeting of "humanitarian aid workers and UN observers," its causing of ecological disasters, etc.), and opts for the one-state solution beloved of closet antisemites. Or poet Aharon Shabtai who in his volume *J'Accuse* vilifies Israeli soldiers as killers from the egg. Or author Shlomo Sand, celebrated in Europe for his recently published *The Invention of the Jews* which argues that the Jewish "nation" is a late social construct without historical or biblical warrant. Or Kenneth Roth, former executive director of *Human Rights Watch*, who solicits funds from the Saudis and flagrantly tilts HRW reports to excoriate Israel and "parrot Palestinian testimonies." Or filmmaker Shimon Dotan whose documentary *Hot House* sympathetically profiles Palestinian terrorist Ahlam Tamini who murdered fifteen Israelis, eight of them children. Or the leftist daily *Haaretz*'s literary critic and belletrist Yitzhak Laor who champions the late, fiercely anti-Israeli Palestinian laureate Mahmoud Darwish (who compares Jews to "flying insects") and who considers Israel as a country fighting a "dirty war," a killer of "unarmed Palestinians." Or Middle East prof Mark LeVine who believes Israel needs to be saved from itself and that the Gaza war was unjustified, and cites highly contaminated sources like "a joint Tel Aviv University-European study," a Hamas spokesman in the *Los Angeles Times*, the *United Nations Re-*

lief and Works Agency (UNRWA), revisionist Avi Shlaim, *Haaretz* Israel-bashing lefties Gideon Levy and Amira Haas, and of course the redoubtable Neve Gordon, to support his bias. Of despicables like Noam Chomsky, Norman Finkelstein, Naomi Klein and Ilan Pappe, nothing more need be said; the very names are sufficient.

Perhaps the worst of this lot, in terms of the empirical harm done to the Jewish state and by extension to Diaspora Jews as well, is the South African jurist Richard Goldstone, crouching like a spider at the center of a UN web of lies. On September 16, 2009, Goldstone tabled his United Nations Report on Israeli conduct during Operation Cast Lead, accusing Israel of crimes it did not commit while effectively exculpating Hamas for crimes it did. Goldstone's strategy was initially to establish a moral equivalence between a country defending its citizens and a terrorist organization deliberately attacking that country's civilians. As one delves deeper into the Report, the strategy becomes ever more insidious, presenting Israel and Hamas not merely as moral equivalents but as political incompatibles, that is, Israel is depicted as a terrorist regime and Hamas as a legitimate government. Goldstone also implied that Israel, but not Hamas, might be referred to the International Criminal Court. In the words of Alan Dershowitz, with reference to the breaking scandal of Goldstone's apartheid past as a white South African hanging judge, "Goldstone is an ambitious opportunist … He has always put personal advancement over principle." With Jews like Goldstone, who needs antisemites?

All of these "haraites," if I may coin a word, have profited in one way or another from their moral delinquency, basking in public renown, cashing in on book sales and lecture fees, furthering their careers and assuming positions of public or institutional importance. Apostasy pays.

The constituency of the ignorant, the negligent, the indifferent and the apathetic is no less vast. The third *yetzer* is ubiquitous among the Jewish population at large but flourishes most conspicuously on university campuses. Leading the charge of the Israel-divestiture movement at UC Berkeley, to take a representative instance, is the Jewish group *Kesher Enoshi* which, as former head of the Intelligence Studies Section of the International Studies Association Abraham Miller writes, "partners with the virulently anti-Zionist group Students for Justice in Palestine." Moreover, "fully one-third of the Jewish Studies program faculty signed a petition on behalf of the divestiture resolution." Even *Berkeley Hillel* has become problematic, "showcasing … Israel-bashing groups." Jewish apathy, he continues, along with Jewish left-wing politics, promotes the Palestinian narrative while prejudicing the Zionist future. Similarly, as Daniel Gordis, president of the Jerusalem Shalem Center, says of Brandeis University's Jewish students who objected to Israel's ambassador Michael Oren delivering a commencement address, "one is struck by an astounding simplicity, and frankly, an utter lack of courage to stand firm against the tidal wave of unbridled hostility toward Israel." As of this writing, the latest instance of such moral and intellectual turpitude comes from the University of Michigan.

These students are enormously energetic in pursuing their project of delegitimizing the Zionist experiment which is Israel, but they are nonetheless totally apathetic in undertaking the quest for truth, that is, the effort to disambiguate the historical and legal facts stifled beneath the many layers of propaganda to which they readily succumb. A moribund curiosity and a lack of enthusiasm for real scholarship are infallible symptoms of intellectual lassitude. These students are obviously bright *in their way*, no doubt excelling at their studies, yet the simplicity of mind is also startling in their failure to recognize how they are ultimately delegitimizing *themselves*. Apathy and simple-mindedness together constitute the third *yetzer*, the inclination to ignorance, of which these campus Jews are the chief carriers and the heralds of things to come.

These three categories of desolation will overlap to some extent. In which bracket does one locate the plethora of anti-Zionist Jewish organizations, like *J Street*, the *New Israel Fund*, the *Committee on New Alternatives in the Middle East*, the *Union for Progressive Zionists*, the *Israel Policy Forum*, the *Jewish Alliance for Justice and Peace (Brit Tzedek V'Shalom)*, *Rabbis for Human Rights*, *Gisha*, *Peace Now*, *B'Tselem*, *Tikkun Olam*, *Choice (Breira)*, the *Canadian Council for Israel and Jewish Advocacy,* the *Canadian Centre for Israel and Jewish Affairs, Independent Jewish Voices,* the *Anti-Defamation League,* the *Union for Reform Judaism,* and *JCall,* among hundreds of simulacra? Some of their members will be motivated by what they regard as a higher vocation, generally of a leftist stamp, others are in the game to advance their own narrow interests, and still others have little idea of the consequences of their lobbying. But like their assorted compatriots, they too are tarred by the promiscuous *yetzer* brush.

I have presented merely a random sampling from all sides of the *yetzer* divide—scientists, philosophers, poets, sophists, casuists, professors, students, organizers, the whole *megilla*. What they all share in various degrees is a specialized intelligence that generates proficiency in their respective fields. But they have something else in common too, namely, an inability to connect with the reality of a world that has rarely managed to welcome or accommodate the Jew in its midst. What is missing here is *ordinary smarts*.

There are, of course, exemplary figures blessed with prodigies of (un)common sense and worldly perceptiveness, from, say, the great Halachic scholar Elijah ben Shlomo Zalman (the Vilna Gaon) for whom secular knowledge, particularly history and geography, were paramount concerns, the founder of the Zionist movement Theodor Herzl, and my kinsman Joseph Soloveitchik whose *The Lonely Man of Faith* provides guidance for the faithful, to contemporary political writers like Caroline Glick, Sarah Honig, the late Barry Rubin, David Horowitz and Dennis Prager, among others. I suspect they comprise the exceptions. But for so many Jews, both among the acclaimed and the general public, an education in the ways of the world is a *sine qua non*. And especially for Jews distracted by the *yetzerim*—even the admittedly noble *yetzer hatov*—such an education would enable them to adopt the necessary strategies for survival, to wit, waking consciousness, group solidarity and a belated awareness that the state of the Jews is inseparable from the Jewish state.

How to acquire this education, this inclination to worldly knowledge and pragmatic intelligence—let us call it the *yetzer hada'at* (sharpening, attention, reflection, rejoicing), mentioned in *Proverbs* 22:17, *Exodus* 18:9, and *Psalm* 26:7? This is the most essential impulse of all. One thing is certain. Knowledge of the temporal domains of history, politics and culture, and of *one's place in the unfolding drama of human relations*, is the ground of perseverance. Only thus can Jews, subject to the enchantments of rootless exaltations, venal self-aggrandizement and congenial mental indolence, finally repudiate the derisory pageant of the foolish, the contemptible and the ignorant. For moral and intellectual redemption is the condition of communal survival.

6

THE RETURN OF
THE PRODIGAL

I grew up in a Jewish anti-Jewish household dominated by my father who never once attended synagogue
and refused to associate with any of the Jewish inhabitants of the town we lived in. My father hated Jews
with a passion—although I should mention that he hated just about everybody with a passion. Jews, however,
for reasons I could never fathom, received an extra share
of his animadversion. Perhaps this was because, despite
his overweening selfishness and high self-esteem, he also
detested himself and simply acted out the venerable cliché, going through the motions of classic psychological
projection. He was not a lovable man. But whatever the
deep interior motive at work in his lava-spewing psyche, I
was taught to regard my fellow Jews with unwavering suspicion. My father was not a leftist, so there was nothing
"red diaperish" about my early education. I learned only
that Jews of any stripe—left or right, observant or secu-

lar—were to be avoided.

But even without such indoctrination, I was ripe for apostasy. I naturally disliked Jewish cooking. The sound of Yiddish was like gristle in my ears. The complacent and self-important worshippers I mingled with during my occasional visits to the synagogue left me cold. With only a few exceptions, I could not tolerate my Jewish relatives. I lived in fear of my uncle Snetzi, who would suddenly rush into the house and fling himself under a bed, whimpering, "They're after me, they're after me." My uncle Aby was a good-natured philanderer who never had a serious thought in his life. Eventually he suffered an aneurism and spent his days shambling aimlessly about the streets, grinning inanely. My auntie Rosie, during her occasional descents upon our hospitality, would install herself in the bathroom and spend long, devoted hours rinsing out her lingerie, over and over again, like a working-class Lady Macbeth fascinated by invisible spots. My auntie Ida was partial to oily slabs of carp wrapped in greasy newspapers, which she would serve up at indigestible dinners. What had I to do with these people, I used to wonder. I was a Jew and yet I wasn't.

The circumcision rite had to be performed on the sly, thanks to the fortunate collusion between my mother—herself the daughter of a long line of rabbis—and the *mohel* conspiring behind my father's back. I was given Hebrew lessons as a child during one of those rare peri-

ods when my father accommodated my mother's wishes. Regrettably, this interval lasted only a short while—
though long enough for me to pick up the rudiments. But
I never had a Bar Mitzvah. Instead of attending Hebrew
School to simulate what passed for correct pronunciation
and learn my prayers (for the most part, phonetically), a
chore my mother insisted upon despite my father's glow-
ering disapproval (this was the only other concession he
ever made to her), I would stop off to play hockey with
my schoolmates on my way to the synagogue. After several months of such enjoyable truancy, the rabbi belatedly
telephoned my mother to inquire as to my whereabouts,
but by then it was far too late to catch up. My mother was
mortified and my father was euphoric. I continued to play
hockey and though I'd devolved into a bad Jew, I evolved
into a pretty good goaltender.

Later on, during my university days and for many
years thereafter, I grew somewhat more sophisticated in
my anti-Jewishness, adopting the political positions favored by the anti-Zionists. I was perfectly aware that for
many of the people I knew, anti-Zionism was merely an
expedient substitution for antisemitism, but I persisted
nevertheless. My father had died but I carried on the family tradition, or at least his side of it.

I was in sync with Hannah Arendt's supercilious disdain of the *Ostjuden* (Eastern European Jews) whom she
regarded as lower-class banausics. Had the BDS scandal,

or the Apartheid Week orgies, or the "peace" NGOs existed then, I would probably have participated in their malignant festivities. I was so fervently pro-Palestinian that my mother disinherited me. I would not have thought to question the pseudo-history of an indigenous Palestinian people who presumably formed a long-established nation, a microbial fable and, in the words of Middle East scholar David Meir-Levi, a "pernicious tradition to which more and more of our mainstream media and academia fall prey." And I would have approved Benny Morris' revisionist libel of Zionism in *Righteous Victims* as a "colonizing and expansionist ideology," rather than affirmed it for what it really was and is, a legitimate, historical movement to reclaim, re-establish and perpetuate the allodial legacy of the Jewish people in the land of their fathers, as I do now. I might even have worn a keffiyeh rather than a kippa. It would have been "the thing to do" and would have confirmed me in my recidivism, aside from allowing me to remain in good standing with the aristocracy of the like-minded. I was certainly no paragon of *sechel*, the partly untranslatable Yiddish word—Saul Bellow's favorite—usually rendered as "smarts."

The shock to my system and to my congenial beliefs came with 9/11, which represented my personal crossing of the Red Sea from the captivity of unreflected notions and crude prejudice to the freedom of real, independent thinking and impartial research. I was at that historic moment trapped on a small Greek island with no way of leaving since all maritime transportation had been suspended. I gradually understood this situation as an allegory of my own prior state of mind, snared in an insular delusion without the intellectual means of deliverance or extrication.

For the next several weeks, stunned by the images I had seen on the television screen in the village café, I submitted myself to a relentless analysis of the values and convictions I had accepted as gospel. How solidly grounded in authentic knowledge were the political convictions I habitually expressed? What were the sources of my attitudes, ideas and judgments? Why was I almost instinctively anti-Israeli in my sentiments? Why did I wish to reject my kinship with Jewish thought, Jewish communion, Jewish antiquity? Why did I march in my thoughts with the Palestinians, the anti-globalists, the welfare socialists, the Peace Now movement? Was I somehow complicit with the demonic forces that wished to bring down America and destroy Israel, that worked against my own survival and the survival of those I loved? Did I really want to become like my father? Could I be so easily brainwashed? What the hell was wrong with me?

They were not Jews who brought down the Twin Towers, but the very people I and my cohort had empathized with. These were the people responsible for the Munich massacre, for myriad airplane hijackings, for suicide bombings, for random acts of terrorism, for the slaughter of innocents, which we had risibly explained away as legitimate acts of "resistance" against the "Zionist entity" and the American hegemon, as expressions of the quest for freedom and justice. In the wake of the 9/11 cataclysm, such frivolous justifications would no longer hold up to scrutiny. New York had been the current target. The next might be Montreal where I lived, or London, or Paris, or Tel Aviv.

I came to the conclusion that I had felt and acted out of mere rote behavior and fortuitous conjecture, out of an unexamined desire to think in accordance with the inferences and presuppositions of my friends, peers and colleagues, my intellectual contemporaries, who were all either members of the international Left or, at any rate, exhibited leftist inclinations. We had embraced the multicultural pieties of the era, were duly anti-colonialist, anti-corporatist, anti-American, and obviously anti-Zionist.

Many of these social paladins and millennial protagonists bivouac'd comfortably in university departments, upscale condos and tony suburban neighborhoods. Their Molotov cocktails were the proverbial lattes over which they would discuss their resonating ideals, plan politically biased academic courses, deplore Islamophobia (even before the factoid), raise consciousness of the plight of the Palestinians and the machinations of the Israelis, and in effect conspire against the very democratic institutions and cultural norms that provided them with the sinecures they blithely took for granted. To my everlasting shame, though I did not go to the same lengths, I hobnobbed with professors in the English Department who would teach their courses from the standpoint of an irreal utopianism, believing in the freedom and autonomy of the aesthetic perspective on life as a prototype of human possibility in a harmonious and compassionate world. This meant a collectivist future without America and certainly without Israel. They had no difficulty surrendering their intellects to such puerile and noxious fantasies. And they had no idea that they were eventually in for a very bumpy ride that would send their double-doubles all over the upholstery.

It is not all that different today. When not slamming capitalism, the free market and the economic infrastructure that pays their salary, they are busy meddling in Israeli affairs. Even as I write, the members of the left-oriented Faculty Association of my former college, executing a hypothetical mandate for which they have neither expertise nor authority and utterly oblivious to the historical record as well as the decrees of international law, are indefatigably circulating anti-Israel propaganda and joining with those who seek to ostracize the Jewish state. The job for which they were elected was to represent a group of teachers in issues relating to working conditions and contractual negotiations with the local Administration, not to involve themselves in affairs for which they were not qualified and which remain completely outside their proper purview. It is rather curious that they had and have no compunction in abusing their remit and ululating along with those who wish to destroy a foreign nation, one in which they have no skin in the game. The quackery and bad faith, indeed, the unctuous stupidity, is almost beyond moral and rational conceiving.

All this was already prefigured in the political climate of ten and twenty years ago. For a considerable while I was a peripheral part of such benighted and hypocritical symposia. As I reflected on the nature of my previous affiliations, I recognized that we were, quite simply, credulous fools. And the anti-Zionist Jews were the worst fools of all. For no matter what lengths of disavowal they might go to, no matter how earnest or cunning or unscrupulous they might be in their collaboration with the enemies of the Jewish state, they were also in the firing line and would not be spared should worse come to worst. They could not believe in, had no conception of, human evil. I am reminded of a passage in Leon Kahn's harrowing memoir of Jewish life in Lithuania during the countdown to the Nazi invasion (and after) *No Time to Mourn*. Kahn describes the inability of the Jewish townspeople to credit the warnings they had received and to gauge the intentions of the enemy that would soon lead to the wholesale slaughter of entire villages. "We could not believe that 'civilized' men could perpetrate [such] horror," he writes. We cannot play dumb. As Israel comes increasingly under attack, so does every Jew in the diaspora, where, as history instructs, there is no perduring guarantee of security.

Perhaps George Steiner said it best in *Language and Silence*: "If Israel were to be destroyed, no Jew would escape unscathed. The shock of failure, the need and harrying of those seeking refuge, would reach out to implicate even the most indifferent, the most anti-Zionist." Israel's fate is, in the last analysis, the fate of every Jew. Rabbi Berel Wein, director of the *Destiny Foundation*, is also right when he reminds us that the conflict in the Holy Land is not "a nice modern day dispute that lends itself to creative diplomacy" but is "in reality a biblical epic" that has "hardened over centuries." A biblical epic is not a political soap opera. Rabbi Wein has expressed a harsh but necessary certitude, and concludes by citing the Talmud which teaches the restorative obligation of "seeing a problem realistically and without wishful thinking and false assessments."

A fresh point of view was plainly necessary. I would have to give myself over to genuine study and to check my susceptibility to the infectious notions that percolated in the atmosphere of the times. I would have to remember anew that as a Jew I was and always would be at risk. As Anglican minister and scholar William Nicholls wrote in *Christian Antisemitism: A History of Hate*, "The forces that led to the Holocaust are still active. Until they are identified and eliminated from society, there is no enduring safety for Jews." It behooved me not only to acquire a deeper familiarity with my own tradition, but with the subtle and not-so-subtle maneuverings of the antisemitic Left if I was not to fall terminally prey to the imbecility and subliminal bloodthirstiness of my presumptive friends. I could no longer consort with a sodality of self-infatuated intellectuals so naively and fecklessly allied with the terrorists, so prone to appeasing evil.

Even more surprising, I came to realize that I was a Jew even as I learned to disown my heritage during the years when I found the question entirely irrelevant to my existence. I see now that this is a deep and self-conflicted aversion the Jew must labor to surmount if he is ever to become whole. What one dislikes in the Jew is only what one dislikes in other people but makes the Jew the repository of, especially if the caviler is a Jew in revolt from his suspected "essence" and who expels himself from his own community. Clearly, this auto-expulsion can take many forms. It can lead to assimilation or conversion, as with the celebrated Russian poet Osip Mandelstam who derided almost everything Jewish, fled from the perceived stigma of lower-class Ashkenazi life and converted from Judaism to Christianity, as we learn from his quasi-autobiography, *The Noise of Time*. It may express itself as a braying renunciation of Zionism and the Jewish state. It can manifest as a process of psychological antisepsis in which the "self-loathing" Jew tries to expunge the effigy with which he has come to be identified.

Such notions are amply documented in what Sander Gilman in *Jewish Self-Hatred* (titled after Theodor Lessing's seminal 1933 book) calls the "historiography of self-hatred," a lengthy chronicle of Jews committed to "altering their sense of self," to neutralizing the power of the demeaning cultural stereotype of the Jew "as if it were a valid set of descriptive categories," and to becoming "what they wish themselves to be." Of course, some observers have claimed that the term "Jewish self-hatred" is misleading and platitudinous—the serpentine Anthony Lerman writing in the *Jewish Quarterly* (Number 210) regards it as "bankrupt" and a form of "demonizing rhetoric." Others with a taste for satire say that those to whom it has been applied are actually "Jewish self-lovers," that is, people who love themselves, their appetites and conceits, more than they cherish the virtues of honor or dignity or loyalty or truth. Perhaps, but the term seems to me accurate enough for, as Gilman points out, such people are in reaction against the social perception of what counts as "typically Jewish," an image with which they have inwardly identified but are determined to annul. They will do everything possible to expunge the twilit awareness of their inner Jew.

Speaking of leftist Jews in particular, Israeli novelist Benjamin Kerstein, who at one time belonged to this perverse school of thought and behavior, confides that "we were taught to be essentially self-hating. If we didn't hate ourselves and hate Israel, we were told that we were racist." Young people indoctrinated in this way are the victims of "psychological abuse" and their preceptors subject to a kind of "auto-totalitarianism." For Kerstein, such reflexive loathing is nothing short of a "psychosis." And there can be no doubt that this is a specifically Jewish phenomenon. Who ever heard of a self-hating Muslim?

True, nonviolent activist Murad Bustami ironically titles an article for *Common Ground News Service* "A 'Self-Hating' Palestinian?" which is not intended seriously. Bustami believes that "resistance" should be conducted peacefully, which puts him at odds with his fellows. In a rather different vein, *Chronikler* journalist Khaled Diab facetiously refers to himself as a self-hating Arab, but he doesn't mean it for a second. In a rather silly and self-serving article on the subject, Diab gets the concept of self-hatred totally upside-down, asserting that "many of the people who fire off accusations of self-loathing are usually self-righteous" and that "the only thing these alleged self-loathers hate is injustice ... and ... should, instead, be called justice lovers." I can think of no better way to justify cowardice and betrayal than to mount an argument like Diab's or Lerman's.

Most deceptively, this spiritual deformation can manifest as a presumed endorsement of the "universal

values" of the Jewish faith at the expense of the particular value of staying alive—a peculiar form of transfer-
ence. Naturally, such recreants and especially Jewish critics of Israel will cover their tracks by arguing, as Canadian
columnist Robert Fulford put it, "that they are [Israel's]
best friends, urging it toward a higher moral position," as
if a country that tolerates Arab anti-Zionists in the Knes-
set, treats its enemies in its hospitals (180,000 in one year
alone), sacrifices its soldiers to avoid civilian casualties in
anti-terror operations (as in Jenin) and showers leaflets on
potential targets (as in Gaza) did not already stake out a
"higher moral position."

Further, such preachments may lead to self-immolation and the embrace of killer ideologies. Thus, we may
be reminded by our ostensible betters of the exhortation
from *Deuteronomy* 10:19, "Love ye therefore the stranger" —even if that stranger has his sights set on your life
and the obliteration of your family. But we are supposed
to show sympathy and understanding for his difficult circumstances as he schemes our destruction. We are urged
to engage in "dialogue," to make concessions, to acknowledge the misery of those who desire one's extinction, to
provide an example of disinterested righteousness for
the rest of humanity. One recalls the great Jewish patriot
Ze'ev Jabotinsky writing about the deluded Jews in Old
Russia who, during the disturbances of the time, "considered it their duty to support the autonomist efforts

of their enemy, on the ground that autonomy is a sacred cause." The upshot? "Jewish heads are smashed." "This sort of thing," he continues, "is not morality, it is twaddle."

Today, such twaddle will often come from *Golus* Jews who live in comfort and enjoy the luxury of exalted rumination, or as we have noted, even from Israelis, almost universally of the Left, who linger in an alternate reality. "There are those," writes Deputy News Editor of *The Jerusalem Post*, Israel Kasnett, "who claim they must save Israel from itself ... if only Israelis," he urges, "would see through the Left's prism." What is the ultimate difference, after all, between the ferocious Canadian-Jewish critic of Israel Naomi Klein and the former Israeli justice minister Tzipi Livni, both of whom pursue lucrative careers while sanctimoniously working against the survival of the Jewish state? At the same time, they like to see themselves as laboring virtuously for the benefit of the poor, the downtrodden, the deprived and the excluded, chiefly among their enemies. But this species of moral commutation is only a slippery evasion of conscience, one of the most effective pretexts to be found in the vast App Store of Jewish alibis, subterfuges and extenuations.

What was Arthur Koestler thinking when he remarked in *Promise and Fulfilment* that, for the Jew, treason is the highest form of patriotism? He was surely being ironic—though articulating a bitter, antiphrastic truth.

Such tergiversators were and are guilty of what in Hebrew is called *Chilul HaShem*, defined as a violation of the Lord's command by abandoning or betraying Judaism to enhance one's social status. This was not for me, or at least not any longer. My emotional and intellectual axis had shifted decisively. Although I once shared Mandelstam's asperities, I have come to realize that I was still a Jew when I fatuously disparaged Yiddish as a plebian excuse for a language, refused to observe our defining holidays, and took up the Palestinian cause as a sign of my supposed even-handedness—before I gave myself the trouble to study the issue more closely and arrive at conclusions more in agreement with reality. I was a Jew when I inveighed against the hardening of the arteries associated with *shtetl* piety or excessive halachic orthodoxy and felt a vicarious shame and embarrassment for the sallow and asthenic physical specimens of the Hasidic communities with whom I had nothing in common. I was still a Jew when for a time I rashly accepted the arguments of our intellectual clerisy which in the name of the "community of mankind" sold out its cultural dower to the enemies of civilization—who, it turns out, were and are resolutely anti-Jewish.

And I remain a Jew though unable to say with assurance whether Jewishness can be reduced to a matter of belief, ethnicity, genetics, illusion, duty, allegiance or cultural attitude. After all, what does an Ethiopian Falasha have to do with a Russian émigré or a Chinese votary or an ultra-Orthodox rabbi from Galicia or the Bnei Menashe in India and Myanmar or facile entertainers like Jon Stewart (né Jonathan Stuart Leibowitz) or assimilated bigots like Richard Falk and Richard Goldstone or a sodden philosopher like Martin Buber with mulch for a mind or true heroes like Theodor Herzl and Ze'ev Jabotinsky? It has been said, I believe correctly, that Jews do not share a religion so much as a history, even if that history has been repudiated. In the same way, Jews are always in danger of sharing a particular kind of future—one which those on the Left, and those who have gambled on the shelter of assimilation, censure from recognition.

Moreover, I am a Jew, as I now realize, also because the world will never let me conclude otherwise. Traitors, assimilationists, court Jews, sycophants, basement cowerers, prodigal sons and daughters, Sabbath Jews, men and women of faith, the noble and the contemptible—they may all find themselves at some fateful moment in time splayed in the crosshairs. Ultimately, the dubious among them cannot quibble their way past endemic hostility or fall back on convenient sophistries. My uncle Snetzi was surely on to something. Paranoia may well be the Jew's only sane response to the world's perennial enmity. In the long run, strenuous attempts at forgetting or denial or glossing-over are a losing proposition.

Today, in the midst of the renewed outbreak of

antisemitism around the globe, I have come to accept Freud's affirmation in a speech delivered on the occasion of his seventieth birthday to the B'nai B'rith Lodge in Vienna: "I myself was a Jew, and it always seemed to me not only shameful but downright senseless to deny it." I have come consciously to incorporate Emil Fackenheim's "614th Commandment" which in his major work, *To Mend the World*, he added to the 613 *mitzvot* or commandments contained in the Pentateuch, namely, of not giving Hitler a posthumous victory.

As I wrote in *Hear, O Israel!*, this injunction has become my *Shamash* candle, the "helper candle" used to light the Hanukkah menorah in memory of the miracle of endurance. And even the way I hear spoken Yiddish has changed, so that it now seems to me unaffected, dulcet and *heimische*.

According to Jewish tradition, since I never solemnized a Bar Mitzvah, I am not yet a man. But I hope that I have become a *mensch*.

7

PULLING RABBIS
OUT OF A HAT

At the battle of Thermopylae (translation: the Hot Gates) in 480 B.C., as Herodotus tells it, 300 Spartans, 700 Thespians and 400 Thebans held up the advance of over a million Persians, an act of heroism that led in the course of time to the victory of the Greek alliance over the armies of King Xerxes I. The historian notes that the Spartan and Thespian contingents at Thermopylae did not flinch before the advancing hordes, but the Thebans "stayed against their will," reluctant to face the enormous odds arrayed against them.

Nevertheless, there is every reason to believe that the Greek force under Leonidas might have kept the Persians indefinitely at bay had they not been betrayed by a certain Ephialtes of Trachis. This Ephialtes, says Herodotus, "stirred by the hope of receiving a rich reward at the king's hands, had come to tell him of a pathway which led across the mountain to Thermopylae, by which disclosure he brought destruction on the band of Greeks who had there withstood the barbarians."

Flash forward to 2011, to a different, yet in some ways comparable scenario: the state of Israel surrounded by enemies and defending its own Hot Gates at the crossroads of the Mediterranean and the Middle East, and the Persians in their millions once again armed to the teeth, threatening to "block out the sun" not with arrows, as in the original battle, but with missiles. *Mutatis mutandis*, instead of the 400 Thebans assembled at the pass, we found 400 left-wing rabbis prepared to surrender the gates to the enemy—or, *in effect*, 400 Ephialtes' poised to betray the faith and give succor to those who would rejoice in their misfortune.

Though going back some years, the sordid story of the 400 Rabbis (see *Cross-Currents* for January 27, 2011) is symptomatic of the state of affairs in a large portion of Jewish society. Taking exception to Glenn Beck's demolition of the apostate Jewish billionaire George Soros, the 400 took out a $100,000 ad in the *Wall Street Journal* accusing Beck and Fox News of cheapening the memory of the Holocaust, of making "literally hundreds of on-air references to the Holocaust and Nazis when characterizing people," and for drawing attention to Soros' self-serving behavior as a teenager in Nazi-dominated Hungary.

It would appear, however, that most of these rabbis had never or rarely watched Glenn Beck or Fox News

since their allegations were inaccurate and seemed almost
wholly based on hearsay. Moreover, they were plainly un-
aware that Beck had often encouraged his readers not to
take his word but to investigate the issues for themselves.
Nor did the good rabbis see fit to disclose that the *Jewish
Fund for Justice*, which paid for the ad, is partially bank-
rolled by Soros' Open Society Foundations. Soros, ever
the magician, has no trouble pulling rabbis out of a hat.

Obviously, they were not impressed by the fact that
Beck is a "righteous Gentile" with enormous influence for
good; a stalwart defender of the Jewish state and a scourge
against anti-Semites, while Soros funds unsavory venues
like *Media Matters* and backs the disreputable advocacy
group *J Street*, an outfit that regards Israel with suspicion
and works to further the interests of Palestinian Arabs at
the Jewish state's expense. Soros targets Israel as contributing to antisemitism, scapegoats the Jewish state for the
turbulence in the Middle East, and as an obstacle to peace
and democracy. "The main stumbling block is Israel," Soros wrote in *The Washington Post.* He seeks to discredit *The
American Israel Public Affairs Committee* (AIPAC); believes
"the pro-Israel lobby" is invested in "suppressing diver-
gent views;" blames Israel for "refusing to recognize the
democratically-elected Hamas government" for pursuing
"military escalation;" and subsidized terrorist-defending
lawyers like the infamous Lynne Stewart. One could go
on. No matter. The 400, whether through ignorance or

perfidy or both, proceeded to vilify their protectors and champion their adversaries. Beck bad, Soros good.

But the 400 rabbis should not be seen as a merely insignificant rabble protesting against what they do not understand. Such truancy of conscience is only an instance of a far more comprehensive attitude to the Zionist experiment and the welfare of the beleaguered nation where it has taken root. There is little in the way of *kiruv*, the Hebrew term for "coming near," the practice of drawing Jews closer to Judaism (usually, but not necessarily, Orthodox Judaism). Quite the reverse. As often as not, we observe a sense of radical estrangement from the *yishuv*, the Jewish community in the Holy Land, whose survival is constantly under threat.

Undeterred by existential peril, our "Theban" rabbis and their go their alienating way. These reverend shufflers speak in large measure for the Reform/Reconstructionist denominations, liberal-minded and left-leaning Jews, and social pressure groups that purport to be reasonable and even-handed, that sponsor debates and colloquia weighted toward the Palestinian cause in the interests of "openness" and "fairness," and that treat their declared enemies with forbearance. It's called, variously, interfaith dialogue" or "peace activism" or "social justice," but what it really amounts to is shilling for the other side.

Indeed—to adjust my Herodotean metaphor—if our troop of rabbis had been the 400 men who rode with

Esau to meet Jacob at Peniel, as we learn in *Genesis* 33, they would not have experienced a change of heart and reconciled with the patriarch. They would have accused Jacob of deceit, aggression, self-aggrandizement, unfairness to the surrounding tribes and who knows what other transgressions, and Israel would have been nipped in the bud.

Thus, it is not just a question of Glenn Beck or any other particular individual who may be the object of communal resentment. Ultimately, the 400 rabbis are no less inimical to Israel and to authentic Jewish concerns than the 400 Thebans, who would have preferred not to fight the enemy massing against them, were delinquent to their own cause. More so, actually, since the rabbis have, as it were, fled their post. In this way, they abet the growing international conviction that Israel is a historical mistake and a mendicant state to be boycotted, sanctioned and eventually erased from the map or folded into a Palestinian-dominated bi-national entity.

Interestingly, diffidence did not spare the Thebans from the fate that befell their more courageous compatriots. Those who do not have their heart in the fight go under just like those who are ready to stand and deliver—except that bravery and clear-sightedness will sometimes prevail, absent betrayal. This is a lesson the good rabbis and their communicants might keep in mind. But if worse should ever come to worst, what form of penance or contrition they will exhibit when it is too late does not bear much consideration.

And what, I wonder, would be the Hebrew name for Ephialtes?

8

HEALING THE WORLD

A few years back I was asked to give a talk for the Toronto chapter of the Jewish Motorcycle Association, a riders' club and benevolent organization. Riders came in from practically everywhere—the U.S., Australia, South Africa, Israel, several European countries and, of course, Canada, approximately 900 attendees, many leather-jacketed, tough-looking specimens of Alpha manhood, others, spiffily dressed professionals from New England. I spoke at the Symposium dinner on diverse themes treating of Jewish culture, politics and religion, primarily regarding the biblical and Talmudic concept of Jewish philanthropy, the pressing need to help restore a violent and broken world. (It is no accident that Israeli medical teams are dispatched almost everywhere that disaster strikes or that Israeli doctors tend to wounded Muslim terrorists as they do to their own people.)

The burden of my talk focussed on the Kabbalistic

notion of *Tikkun Olam*, that is, the canonical injunction to repair a fallen world—*Tikkun* means "repair," *Olam*, "for all time"—and the Seven Noahide Laws complementing the Ten Commandments, recognized by the U.S. and ratified by the 102nd Congress as Public Law 102-14.

Briefly, Kabbalah is a mystical philosophy dating back to the 12th Century and formalized by the 16th Century Safed rabbi Isaac Luria, which seeks to explain the nature of the cosmos, man's place and purpose in it, and the esoteric meanings implicit in the Hebrew Bible. One might posit that the Noahide Laws, their inception dating variously from the 2nd Century B.C. to the 2nd Century A.D., which prescribed ritual and moral duties upon the sons of Noah (i.e., Jewish congregants) is the historic and theological precursor of Kabbalah. The Seven Laws are listed in different sequence, depending on which source one consults, but for our purposes it is the traditionally accepted Seventh Law that is most important. The standard formulation of this imperative reads: *Establish courts of law to ensure justice in our world*, thus providing for harmony to be restored to mankind as it conforms to a transcendent order. This is the essence of *Tikkun Olam*.

Nevertheless, *Tikkun Olam* can have harmful effects. The Jewish liberal/left in the U.S., Canada and Israel is so busy saving the world, lobbying for all suffering humanity—especially social and cultural minorities who have little or no sympathy for their benefactors—that it has forgotten that they are themselves always at risk in a world in which anti-Semitism has never died. There have been genocides before and after the Shoah, but these atrocities have largely faded and future generations need not expect a massive racial cleansing.

This is not the case with the world's most irrational and undying hatred. Anti-Semitism is forever, as if embedded in humanity's DNA. This is the fundamental difference to be acknowledged. An Armenian can walk down a street in Amsterdam, Paris, London, Malmo or Berlin without fear; a Jew, not so much. South Africa is no haven. Sweden is a danger zone. Even peaceable Canada has its pockets of anti-Jewish sentiment.

The U.S. is no exception. Troops of Louis Farrakhans can spring up anywhere. Keith Ellison was Deputy Chair of the DNC. Alexandria Ocasio-Cortez is closely associated with Jew-baiting Thomas Lopez-Pierre, he of "greedy Jewish landlords" fame. As Karin McQuillan pointed out in *American Thinker*, "She hates Israel and supports Muslim terrorists, whom she compares to Muslim protesters in Ferguson." Other Democrats such as Ilhan Omar, Linda Sarsour, Scott Wallace and Leslie Cockburn have joined the anti-Semitic hate fest. "How much of this," McQuillan asked rhetorically, "will mainstream Jewish Democrats … be willing to swallow?" Such evils have to be expected and constantly challenged. Indeed, the alt-Left (which is now the Left almost *in toto*) is typically anti-Semitic, anti-Israel and, of course, anti-American. Cut Israel down to size. Make America Grim Again.

My counsel to the conferees was simple: be always vigilant, consider yourselves and your families first, and only then worry about the world. *Tikkun Olam* is all fine and dandy, but to set that messianic task before the imperative of self-preservation is foolishness personified—or as we say in Yiddish, *gantz meshugàs.* The many Jews enamored of the socialist and communist ideologies of their progressivist colleagues are a testimony not only to their folly but to the power of certain scriptural precepts—especially to the influence of Talmudic exhortation and the Book of the prophet Amos, which inveighs against those indifferent to the plight of the disadvantaged, yet does not distinguish earned prosperity from crass exploitation. As I argued, the world you want to save does not necessarily love you. Therefore, stay alert and temper your ideological extravagances. Don't listen to me if you are offended, I conceded, but at least consider your wives and children. Almost immediately, the entire New York assembly rose to a man and conspicuously walked out.

Naturally, I was initially taken aback, but the mass exodus only served to reinforce my fears, for it was clear they were far too mesmerized by the principle of *Tikkun Olam* to take its dark side into account. The Jewish preoccupation with repairing the world, with little regard to the possibility of future cataclysms or isolated evils, is a species of sanctimonious negligence. Jewish leftism may be understandable, which does not prevent it from being the height of naivety and ultimately ruinous.

～

But we are not dealing with an exclusively Jewish problem. The Judeo-Christian West is also in thrall to *Tikkun Olam* and is assiduously working against its own interests, having welcomed a calamitous inundation of adverse cultures, including murderers, rapists, marauders and economic parasites, into its midst. Helping the stranger is an exalted mission but, applied uncritically, it can have devastating effects, as is evident from the vast influx of unreconstructed refugees and jihadists swarming in great numbers into Western nations.

A report from the RAND Corporation revealed the enormous and unsustainable cost of this domestic invasion. Along with the destructive and bloody terror attacks visited regularly upon host nations and the consequent disruption of civil life, it is estimated "that since 2004, terrorism has cost the EU about €185 billion in lost Gross Domestic Product (GDP) and around €5.6 billion in lost lives, injuries, and damage to infrastructure. It is argued that terrorism also harms trade, foreign direct investment and tourism...as well as transport." The cost continues to mount. As for "merrie olde England," it is pretty well cooked.

The U.S. and my own country, Canada, are by no

means exempt from the economic and demographic catastrophe that awaits them as a result of such migration and refugee flows. Kaye Forest and Sierra Rayne, in an *American Thinker* article analyzing the RAND report, go one better than did Donald Trump in advocating "a *complete* moratorium on further immigration from the geographies and ideologies of concern." Similarly, in the words of Michael Walsh, "The issue of 'immigration' has now reached a critical mass on both sides of the Atlantic, with Latin Americans marching on the U.S. across the southern border and mostly Muslim 'migrants' trekking to the European version of El Norte—France, Germany, and England." As we reach the inflection point, assuming we have not yet passed it, the effect of celebrating the "diversity" and "tolerance" canard is to bring "the civilized First World down to the nasty, brutish level" of the Third World.

So much for policy-driven compassion and magnanimity, principles which are now being re-thought and reversed by various nations and affected regions—Italy, Spain, Austria, and the Visogràd Group. The Noahide Laws, specifically the Seventh, and *Tikkun Olam* have not healed the world, though it will have benefitted the alien and often hostile cultures that have installed themselves among us. A noble cause can be lethal. Of course, the cause is not always noble. *Tikkun Olam* will also be used as a cover for cynical or corrupt pursuits, to facilitate a globalist ideology or party voting prospects.

Nonetheless, one thing is clear. Whether in the Jewish community in particular or the Judeo-Christian West as a whole, programmatic solicitude for the fugitive, the disadvantaged and the suffering of other nations and cultures can, *if not properly monitored*, wreak havoc and perhaps lasting damage on our societies. It is not as if we don't have lots of problems of our own—which are only exacerbated by the problems we have imported. Israel and the West make common cause. As Jonathan Neumann writes in *To Heal the World?*, "From the eschatological perspective, the distinction between particular and universal is collapsed."

There is, in fact, no such thing as "universal humanity" in the sense that we all want the same things. We don't. Some peoples and cultures are manifestly not civilizational partners. If we are determined to extend our concern and hospitality to the afflicted in and from other parts of the world, let us at least ensure that that those we allow into our country share our customs, civics and values, are willing and eager to integrate, and are able to contribute to the well-being and prosperity of the nation. Failing this obligation, we can look forward to increasing levels of social turmoil, cultural fragmentation and economic vandalism—in short, a general decline in both our standard of living and our rules of civil order. Let us hope it is not too late to realize the prohibitive cost of *Tikkun Olam*. The clock is ticking, like a bomb.

9

SPEAKING OF
THE SHOAH

I have always felt that the Holocaust was (and is) *essentially* nonrepresentable for those who did not suffer in the Inferno, an event of such unthinkable consequence and horror that anyone who did not experience it could scarcely claim the right to speak about it. For by doing so we almost inevitably cheapen it, turn it into worn and soiled currency, lapse into unforgivable glibness irrespective of our sincerity or ethical engagement. How can one speak about that which one has not only not undergone but cannot truly imagine? The point was forcefully made by Hannah Arendt in her *Essays in Understanding*, where she articulated her belief that "the ongoing problem—finding a mode of representation adequate to the transgressive nature of the phenomenon which, at the same time, does not fall into mystification—is endemic to the material and perhaps unresolvable." Such indefeasible horror would appear to resist both language and mind—

unless, we might think, one has been reduced to the level of the bestial.

In the words of Bernhard Schlink from *The Reader*, addressing the incommunicable nature of the Holocaust, "We should not believe we can comprehend the incomprehensible, we may not compare the incomparable ... because to inquire is to make the horrors an object of discussion ... instead of accepting them as something in the face of which we can only fall silent in revulsion, shame and guilt." Or as George Steiner put it in an incisive and harrowing essay called "The Long Life of Metaphor," the problem "as to whether there is a human form of language adequate to the conceptualization and understanding of Auschwitz, as to whether the limits of language do not fall short of the limits of the Shoah experience, is now ineradicably installed in Jewish existence." According to Steiner, we are still trying to come to terms with "the exit of God" from language.

Indeed, even God Himself, according to Yiddish poet Simcha Simchovich in a collection appropriately called *Remnant*, may have been unequal to the monstrousness of the event:

> *God Himself hid his face, in panic,*
> *on that day.*

Further, it seems to me that any honest and committed attempt to engage with the reality of the Holocaust, in whatever degree so unscalable an effort is remotely possible, would require one *as a Jew* to change one's life drastically, categorically, irreversibly. Assuming that he or she is somehow capable of assimilating even partially the sheer and brute occurrence of this Inconceivable, how would it then be possible to live in the daily sunlight untouched by the weighty and tenebrous shadow of History? To write poems in defiance of Theodor Adorno's famous dictum that after Auschwitz poetry was no longer possible? To concern ourselves with market brands? To root for the home team? One recalls Rabbi Mordecai Levy of Zemyock's rhetorical question in André Schwarz-Bart's *The Last of the Just*, "And tell me, Brethren, how a truly Jewish heart could laugh in this world?" And yet we do laugh, write poems, attend sports events, and shop happily. Life, as they say, goes on, despite the premonition that those who suffered in the camps might turn from us in posthumous rejection of a contentment masked by occasional professions of anguish and condign donations. The paradox is not easily avoided.

Primo Levi phrases the question with terrible intensity in *Shemá*, a title poem based on the central Jewish prayer "Hear, O Israel", in which he demands of those who "live secure/In your warm houses" and who "return at evening to find/Hot food and friendly faces" to recall the incendiary words in which he brings to mind the cataclysms of Jewish history, words that should be burned into the Jewish soul:

> *Engrave them on your hearts*
> *When you are in your house, when you walk on your way,*
> *When you go to bed, when you rise.*
> *Repeat them to your children.*
> *Or may your house crumble,*
> *Disease render you powerless,*
> *Your offspring avert their faces from you.*

In essence, how can literature and communal speech come to terms with that which resists imaginative and psychological closure? This is very near to the great German-Jewish poet Paul Celan's perhaps unresolvable question: how can language itself escape moral and ideological pollution or manage to convey that which is incommensurate with the conceptual or evocative power of the word? Celan, of course, was thinking of the German language he loved so profoundly but felt had become too morally contaminated to be handled without the prospect of contagion and too intellectually suspect to be used as a medium of reference. The renowned German-Jewish critic Marcel Reich-Ranicki confronted this reductive conundrum in his extensive oeuvre, in particular *The Author of Himself*, by reacting in the opposite way. Rather than paring his words to the bone or ceasing to write altogether, he determined instead to use the German language superbly—as if one could separate a language and a literature from a history and a people.

But with respect to the Holocaust, the question involves *any* medium of representation or reference, any language whatsoever. How can one, in the words of Celan's exegete and translator John Felstiner, "name the eclipse without profaning it"? And as Alan Munston remarks somewhere, the Holocaust "is very difficult to write about, because it requires not the large gesture, but great tact." Yet to what extent is such tact even possible? The acclaimed American-Jewish thriller novelist Daniel Silva in his *A Death in Vienna* opted to rely on a simple descriptive record of life in the camps, a victim's transcript almost devoid of commentary. There is no attempt to purple up the atrocity; spareness suffices. Perhaps this is as close as we can get to "tact"—though even here, the imagination cannot contain the enormity of the unconscionable.

Moreover, the experience of the Holocaust is not only *intrinsically* nonrepresentable in any artistic or discursive medium but must also be recognized *as an inherently Jewish experience* before it can even be approached as one of "universal import," which latter would lead to a more generic and softer form of indignation, dread or loathing. The effort to extend the Holocaust threat to apply potentially to all peoples is dangerously misguided since the only people in the world who have to face the threat of genocide, generation after generation, are the Jews. The Armenians will not face another genocide. The Tutsis (and the Hutus in Burundi before the Rwanda slaughter) need no longer fear the specter of annihilation. Aboriginal societies in the West do not have to worry about another impending wave of extermination.

But for the Jewish people, the prospect of genocide is a menace that never dissipates. Rather than adulterating their concern by pretending to be socially enlightened and flattering themselves on their ostensibly higher calling under the rubric of "social justice," Jews should not make a fetish of universal tolerance when the whole point is particular survival—especially now, not only with regard to the Muslim Middle East but in Europe as well where a conceptual Zyklon B is in the air. The evidence for a renewed, 1930s-like upsurge of antisemitic rhetoric and activity, as noted by reputable commentators like David Hornik, Giulio Meotti, Jonathan Tobin, Robin Shepherd and many others, is starkly undeniable. "European intellectuals may think they operate on a different level from street thugs," writes Tobin, "But the logical next step from the hounding of Jews on the editorial pages and in academia is clear." Shepherd, for his part, is apprehensive that the antisemitic virus may spread to the U.S. The fact remains. "The Holocaust and the anti-Semitism that led to it," writes Ayaan Hirsi Ali, correctly, in *The Caged Virgin*, "cannot be compared to any other form of ethnic cleansing." To fasten on its presumptive universality without first understanding its Jewish dimension is to dilute its singular and interpellant character.

The quandary deepens for the Jew who is, in some mysterious but ineluctable way, morally beholden to those who perished in the camps, as if, as Jews, we feel that *those of us who died died for those of us who didn't*. How does one come to terms with a revelation of such unforgiving magnitude? The tendency is to move in two directions at once, away from the Holocaust through assimilation or sentimental trivializing and toward it in virtue of the compulsion to assuage the guilt of survival and to retrieve or forge an identity from communal suffering. Gershom Scholem put the matter with his customary clarity in his 1963 "Letter to Hannah Arendt" in which he states the contradiction of a people who manifest "on the one hand, a devotion to the things of this world that is near-demonic; on the other, a fundamental uncertainty of orientation in this world." The dilemma of negotiating the relation between wanting to live the good life and needing to remember the evil one is likely insoluble.

The Holocaust will not go away. We are still asking the question, though with renewed urgency, that the Psalmist posed in *Psalm* 44:23-26, "why sleepest thou, O Lord? ... Wherefore hidest thou thy face, and forgettest our affliction and our oppression?" One might also mention Charles Hartshorne's "process theology," the theory of a God Who is mutable and evolving and Who suffers with us in the course of a shared History—which leaves us with an evolutionary Being who just happens to be immortal. Even the most radical fringe of Reform or Reconstructionist Judaism would have trouble defending so thin and undemanding and *humanized* a form of religious faith. Abraham Heschel goes so far as to propose that "Judaism is *God's* quest for man," which tends to encapsulate man within his own historical parentheses, though the argument elaborated in his book *God in Search of Man* cannot, in my estimation, let Divinity off the hook any more than a God subject to Darwinian laws is thereby absolved.

The Hebrew Rabbinate is especially perplexed by the sheer unaccountability of human evil festering beneath an indifferent heaven, although the late Rabbi Ovadia Yosef, Sephardi Chief Rabbi and spiritual head of the Shas Party in Israel, appears to have settled the issue to his satisfaction by deposing that Holocaust victims were the souls of re-embodied Jewish sinners who "had been incarnated to atone." The good Rabbi, it would seem, is merely righting the retributive balance by bringing back the recreants who escaped punishment the first time around to pony up for their transgressions later on. How to explain a million and more innocent children slaughtered by humanoid brutes escapes the rabbi's juridical attention. Rabbi Yosef's egregious, administrative attempt to balance the books should be seen as one more expression, albeit an extreme one, of how the Holocaust in itself, together with the passionate need to justify the ways of God to man (assuming He is not *absconditus*), is fundamentally *the* obdurate and undisclosing fact for Jewish life in our time—that which we are struggling to domesticate.

Thus, the question of theodicy, of whether it is still possible to "assert eternal Providence" in the midst of our contemporary Gehenna, continues to baffle and repel understanding. For the condition of the Jew is precisely the reverse of the little Christian boy's in Chaucer's *Prioress' Tale*, who was murdered by Jews and flung into a cesspit where he persisted miraculously in singing the *Alma Redemptoris*. But the fictive fate of the Christian is the real fate of the Jew, only the question now, in the apparent eclipse of hope and, for many, the imminent death of faith, is how to sing the *Alma Redemptoris* in the face of an absent or detached God or, what is even worse, a God who has capitulated to the void that He could not fill. As Celan writes in one of his strangest poems,

> *"Unoccupiable I":*
> *The Supernothing threw*
> *its lot with me;*
> *all ice,*
> *it gives up the fight*

the word we have turned into currency points up the difficulty of imagining and naming the nature of the cataclysm that could not have occurred under the watchful and custodial gaze of a benevolent Creator.

"Holocaust" originally and properly signified a whole burnt *offering or sacrifice to the gods or to God* and is consequently a disturbing misnomer which capitalizing does little to rectify. (Celan used instead the periphrastic "that which happened," and in his "Conversation in the Mountains" referred to the Lord as *Hearest Thou* and *No One*, the God who does not answer Jewish prayers.) Others will use the standard Hebrew term "Shoah" (calamity)—and others, like this writer, will use the words interchangeably. In effect, the word "Holocaust" is inappropriate whether God exists or not, yet we are constrained to use it in common speech for lack of any other readily comprehensible word to designate what is both unimaginable and ineludible, that which cannot be experienced by proxy or adequately described but which must somehow be confronted and absorbed. Given these factors, an *earned redemption* from the stain of false consciousness may well be beyond the strength and capacity of most of us who live in elegiac proximity to the unspeakable, yet it must be undertaken.

The Jewish philosopher Emmanuel Levinas identifies a strange ontological force or phenomenon that he calls the "there is" (an adaptation of the Heideggerian concept of *Dasein*), something independent of personal initiative, like insomnia or infirmity, which vanquishes and depersonalizes consciousness. "In the maddening experience of 'there is'," Levinas writes in *Ethics and Infinity*, "one has the impression of a total impossibility of escaping it." The Holocaust is the great and inescapable "there is" for Jewish consciousness and life in our time, which insists absolutely that we come to some sort of terms with it. Yet the relationship of the relatively unscathed individual with a collective and tragic history of this amplitude must always be a scalene one, not only because it is unimaginable but because responsibility is not for the self, as Levinas argues, but "initially for the Other. This means that I am responsible for my responsibility." As if this were not enough, this responsibility, Levinas rightly claims, is "untransferable"; it cannot be assumed by another who comes to relieve us of the burden of confrontation or to cleanse us of our sins of omission, let alone those of commission.

As a character in *The Last of the Just* asks, now that the sky has shattered, "If God is in little pieces, what can it mean to be a Jew?" *The Jew remains perpetually vulnerable to the unthinkable—this is what it means to be a Jew.* And for this reason the Holocaust must be remembered, grappled with, revived in thought for all its horror and incommensurability—and for all our deficiencies of character and our paucity of genuine empathy. The "injunction is simply to keep this moment in Jewish history," writes the French-Jewish philosopher Alain Finkielkraut in *The Imaginary Jew*, "so that it does not gradually disappear into oblivion." Forgetfulness may subsidize the ubiquitous drive to extermination to which Jews are always suscepti- ble. The horror must be spoken even if it cannot be tru- ly imagined, even if we feel facile and inadequate before that which we have not suffered, even if it is diminished and falsified as in Norman Finkelstein's reprehensible *The Holocaust Industry*, and even if it remains *fundamentally* in- communicable.

The bottom line is: we still need to talk about what we cannot talk about. We still need to speak the unspeak- able, regardless of our inherent human shallowness and petty infatuations. The indifference of many, both Jews and non-Jews, must be countered, just as the enmity of Islamists, Holocaust-deniers and those apostate Jews who have turned against their own people must be deci- sively checked. As we strain to avoid another cataclysm, the word and the text, the repository of memory, must be kept alive in the face of the unqualifiable. Awareness precedes action. Recollection influences the future. And speech is a prelude to engagement. This is the only way to try to ensure that Never Again does not become Ever Again.

10

THE CHILDREN OF
EDWARD SAID

There is a fascinating passage from the *Koran*, *surah* 101, its initial lines variously translated as "The Disaster! What is the Disaster?" (N.J. Dawood, *The Koran*), "The Crashing Blow. What is the Crashing Blow?" (M.A.S. Abdel Haleem, *The Qur'an*), "The day of Noise and Clamor. What is the day of Noise and Clamor?" (Abdullah Yusuf Ali, *The Meaning of The Holy Qur'an*), and so on. The Arabic term in question, *Al-Qaria*, is also translated as "the Clatterer," giving us the most enigmatic version of all, which can be rendered as "The Clatterer! What is the Clatterer? And what shall teach thee what is the Clatterer?" (See the online version of Abdul Daryabadi). Here below is a very readable reproduction from an Arabic/English Facebook site:

The Clatterer—

what is the Clatterer?
And what teaches thee what the Clatterer is?
The day that men shall be like scattered moths,
and the mountains shall be like carded wool.
Then as for him whose scales are heavy,
he shall be in a pleasing life.
And as for him whose scales are light,
his abode shall be the Abyss.
And what teaches thee what it is?—
A blazing Fire.

Yusuf Ali, whose translation and commentary has come to be regarded by many as definitive, parses this *surah* as referring to the Day of Judgment "when men will be distracted and the landmarks of this world will be lost, but every deed will be weighed in a just balance, and find its real value and setting." Taking the liberty of the infidel, my own reading of surah 101 differs markedly from the canonical interpretation.

Who are the Clatterers? They swarm everywhere in the Western world. Some of these Clatterers are out-and-out bigots who pontificate in the media, the academy and the political arena. We know them well. Others are guilty of what political commentator George Jonas calls "pragmatic anti-Semitism," the trendy form of the pestilence taken on board by opportunistic politicos and fashionable highbrows, "just as it was in the 1930s." Some are "Chatham House" specialists who wish to influence public policy in the direction of a kind of mob-friendly gliberalism. Yet others primarily from the postmodern, multicultural and globalist Left, inspired by the special pleading of the late Edward Said, have espoused the Arab/Muslim/Palestinian cause as inherently virtuous and reasonable.

It is instructive to focus on the primary postulates of Edward Said and his tribe of like-minded post-colonialists. The 1978 publication of Said's *Orientalism* prepared the way for the revisionist climate that governs much of the intellectual thought-world today. It marked a decisive shift in contemporary sentiment in favor of Islam and against the West, which is to say, America, Israel and Zionists. Said's tutelary presence is still everywhere to be found, as we can see in the now-ubiquitous denigration of America, Israel and Zionism and the corresponding rehabilitation of the Arab/Muslim axis and of the Palestinians in particular.

One of Said's major premises is that the Arab world suffers from the West's "simple-minded dichotomy of freedom-loving, democratic Israel and evil, totalitarian, and terroristic Arabs," a distinction which obfuscates "a clear view of what one talks about in talking about the Near East." This is obviously no longer the consensus, but the argument continues to be made for partisan purposes, especially in Middle East Study departments running riot on Western campuses. Said has done his dirty work superbly, reinforcing the canard of the Arabs as merely "a surmountable obstacle to Israel's creation."

Jack Cashill reports that Said served for many years on the Palestine National Conference, "alongside ... Yassir Arafat and still harder core radicals from the Popular Front for the Liberation of Palestine, the terrorist group that hijacked the *Achille Lauro*." True to form, Said there extravagantly praises his friend, Israel Shahak, one of the most viperous Jewish Jew-haters of modern times whose anti-Talmudic and anti-Israeli *Jewish History, Jewish Religion* has made a major contribution toward the effort to disentitle the Jewish state. In any event, it appears that the faux apostolic tradition continues at both the academic and political levels.

To appropriate one of his own images, the impression arises of Said riding into the field of Middle East scholarship like Rudolph Valentino's flamboyant Sheik Ahmed Ban Hassan intent on a rescue mission. Said, himself not a Muslim but a self-proclaimed Christian Palestinian—although it now turns out that, like Yasser Arafat, who claimed to be from East Jerusalem, he was an Egyptian—is the Pied Piper of our current Orientalists and postcolonial mandarins, a public figure whose intellectual respectability and personal charisma have made him a very effective evangelist for the movement.

The problematic nature of his oeuvre seems not to matter. To little avail, Ibn Warraq in *Defending the West* has convincingly shown that *Orientalism* is a veritable tissue of fabrications, misconceptions, internal contradictions, damaging omissions, historical blind spots, false attributions and extremely shabby scholarship, all amounting to what Warraq calls a form of "intellectual terrorism." For all his suavity, Said possessed an intifadic temperament. The famous episode of the Columbia prof chucking stones at Israeli soldiers is only a physical embodiment of his textual lapidations. Ironically, in developing his position, Said condemns Western orientalists for employing "retrograde intellectual tactics," which is precisely what Warraq reveals him to be guilty of.

Arabist Robert Irwin's demolition of Said's "labyrinth of false turns, *trompe l'oeil* perspectives and cul-de-sacs" is no less devastating. In *For Lust of Knowing*, Irwin writes that "the distortion of subject matter in *Orientalism* is so fundamental that to accept its broad framework as something to work with and then correct would be merely to waste one's time." Said's book, he continues, "seems to me to be a work of malignant charlatanry in which it is hard to distinguish honest mistakes from willful misrepresentation."

Apart from Warraq and Irwin, as well as Bernard Lewis in his well-known quarrel with Said, Kanan Makiya (incidentally, no great friend of Israel) in *Cruelty and Silence*, Martin Kramer in *Ivory Towers on Sand* and a seemingly repentant Christopher Hitchins of respected memory, who once collaborated with Said, very few thinkers have had the audacity or the courage to call Said's bluff.

Why have we so capriciously accepted his thesis that the West has worked with prefab stereotypes of the Orient? Why, with few exceptions, have we not investigated how the Orient has assembled an equally illusory straw man of its presumed Western oppressor? (One such exception is furnished by Ian Buruma and Avishai Margolit's *Occidentalism*, dealing with the "dehumanizing picture of the West painted by its enemies.") And why, for that matter, have we waited so long to explode Said's self-perpetuated myth of origins—or to savor the piquant fact, as Cashill conclusively documents in *Hoodwinked* and again in *Deconstructing Obama*, that he was born in a Jewish hospital in Jerusalem where his parents rightly evaluated the odds of a safe delivery? And that Said, whose father was a naturalized American, also held American citizenship from birth, which he had no intention of relinquishing.

Despite the damaging critiques of his work, Said-like thinking has become epidemic among the emir class of intellectual Clatterers. The fact that the Muslim Middle East currently has little to offer the world except lessons in state repression and religious fanaticism and the efficient distribution of bloody, indiscriminate killing techniques seems to have escaped these luminaries almost perfectly. The so-called "Arab Spring" furnished ample evidence that Clatterdom inevitably gets the world wrong: Libya was a bloodbath, Tunisia leaned toward renewed fundamentalism, al-Qaeda made inroads in Yemen, and

Egypt went rogue.

In lionizing Edward Said, popular novelists such as Ahdaf Soueif in her novel *The Map of Love* (the character Omar is a stand-in for Said) and debatable scholars such as Rashid Khalidi, who occupies the Edward Said Chair of Modern Arab Studies at Columbia University, and their peers and colleagues do not advance the cause of truth and understanding but promote culturally vetted stereotypes while adding ever more entries to the pseudodoxia epidemica. The tendency to rely on clichés, unreflected truisms, popular beliefs and what Francis Bacon in *Novum Organum* called "Idols of the Theatre"—faults arising from received systems of thought—should be seen for what it is, a form of intellectual evasion that spares critic, novelist or scholar from having to study the relevant issues independently, outside the dispensary of commonplace assumptions. It should be more than enough to downgrade their intellectual credit rating.

John Esposito, director of the Prince Alwaleel Bin Talal Center for Muslim-Christian Understanding at Georgetown University, deserves special mention as a lineal descendent of Said's. Esposito writes in his co-edited volume *Islam and Democracy* that "[i]t is important to examine the conceptual resources within Islam for democratization" and to see that "the term 'democracy' is capable of multiple interpretations and applications." Esposito's "democracies" are like Groucho Marx's "principles": "If you don't like them, I have others." The fact that there is no true democracy anywhere in the Islamic world, not even in Indonesia or Turkey which were frequently cited as democratic beacons and signs of the reformability of Islam, does not constitute a problem for someone who is funded by Qatari and Saudi money—no more than it did for Jimmy Carter whose Peace Center floats on Wahhabi cash.

Esposito has assumed the mantle of Edward Said to become Senior Academic Clatterer among today's pro-Islamic intellectual synod. In *The Future of Islam*, he asserts against all the evidence that "religion will remain a significant political and social force for reform" and endorses the convenient fiction that serves the interests of Western temporizers, namely that the "threat to the West will not come from civilizational differences but from the political and socioeconomic reality that breeds radicalism." The degree of cognitive dissonance exemplified by such statements, however typical of our Islamic infatuates, paid proselytizers and professional flunkies, is really quite remarkable. Obviously infected by what Bernard Lewis in a 1954 essay for The Royal Institute of International Affairs called "the romantic and apologetic presentation of Islam" that discounts the fact that "the political history of Islam is one of almost unrelieved autocracy," Esposito concludes by stressing our "shared values, dreams and aspirations."

Indeed, no catalogue of Said's innumerable acolytes would be complete without mentioning Barack Obama. The once Clatterer-in-Chief studied under Said at Columbia in the period between 1981 and 1983, taking at least one course from his presumptive mentor. He was later photographed with him, seated at the same table and engaged in earnest conversation at a 1998 Arab American Action Network dinner in Chicago, where Said delivered the keynote speech calling, as a news account has it, for a campaign "against Israeli apartheid." Being someone's dinner companion is not an offense. But when that "someone" is Edward Said, a former preceptor, a pro-Arab and anti-Israeli firebrand, about to give a scandalous address, there is room for suspicion.

As Andrew McCarthy wrote in *National Review Online*, "Obama plainly maintained some sort of tie with Said," whose intimate circle also included Obama's friends, Weather Underground terrorists Bill Ayers and Bernadine Dohrn, and Rashid Khalidi. Dinesh D'Souza in *The Roots of Obama's Rage* points out that Said "seems to have had a lasting influence on Obama: some of Obama's writings are highly resonant with Said's themes and arguments." And Stanley Kurtz, author of *Radical-in Chief*, for his part sees "a sincere interest in Said's radical views." True, the details of the relation ... remain somewhat shrouded since Obama has steadfastly refused to release his Columbia transcripts and his graduating thesis—a suppression which also generates suspicion.

The question now presents itself. What stance should the justly skeptical take up? How we should properly respond to our Clatterers is not that difficult to determine. They should be read or attended to not with the proverbial grain of salt but the entire salt mine. Their strictures and admonitions invariably mislead and can be counted on to exacerbate a deteriorating political situation. Emerging from the ambience of *Orientalism*, some consciously, others unconsciously, the Clatterers swivel between disingenuousness and blindness. Their "scales are light" and the verdict of history will be pronounced against them. It is only a matter of time.

11

THE SCOURGE OF
JEWISH SELF-DIVISION

I have often felt sometimes bemused, sometimes incensed, about what is surely the strangest fact of Jewish life, namely, its self-division. Since time immemorial, the Jewish people have been at war with themselves, both in the Holy Land and the Diaspora, allowing themselves to succumb to one of history's most mordant ironies. In turning against themselves, they have effectively collaborated with those who would suppress, conquer or extinguish the Jewish community.

The template was already established in the Book of Genesis, where we read how one brother slew another in jealousy and resentment and a group of conspiratorial brothers sold their sibling into slavery. From that point on, the biblical archive presents a saga of recrimination, envy, hatred and fratricidal strife that in different degrees has imperiled the very survival of the Jewish "nation." The pattern was consolidated in the story of Korah, Dathan and Abiram, the three rebels who "rose up" before Moses and challenged his authority. As the Lord said to Moses, "I have seen these people, and, behold, it is a stiffnecked people." (*Exodus* 32:9)

Brother against brother, prophet against people, idolatrous kings and priests against these very prophets, and even nation against nation form an indelible part of the Jewish chronicle. The history of the Two Kingdoms provides a continuingly relevant object lesson. After the death of King Solomon, the Israelite communality broke apart into the two warring monarchies of Israel and Judah. The shedding of kinship blood critically weakened the two kingdoms, leading to the conquest of Israel by the Assyrians and the reduction of Judah first by the Chaldeans, then by the Egyptians, and finally by the Babylonians.

The Jewish epic across the wilderness of history may be described as: *divide and be conquered. Surah* 59:14 of the *Koran* tells us something very true about us Jews: "There is much hostility between them: their hearts are divided … " It seems that the wise counsel of Maimonides in the *Mishneh Torah* has no resonance for the backsliders: "All of Israel and those who are joined to it are to each other like brothers. If brother shows no compassion to brother, who will show compassion to him?"

Who, indeed? We see the sorry spectacle of division acting itself out today in the violent civil protests against

Prime Minister Benjamin Netanyahu's efforts to reform a hard-core, *self-appointing*, Leftist Supreme Court, which regularly thwarts the will of legitimate right-wing governments. It was on this platform that Netanyahu was elected by a massive majority of the vote. But the Left is good at civil disruption. There have been resignations and firings of dissident members of the government and raging animosity against the prime minister for his perceived temerity in trying to overhaul the judicial system and redress a long-festering political sore. The Left is having none of it. Netanyahu's critics argue that the plan is pushing Israel down a path to autocracy, a path they themselves appear to be treading. What we are observing, in my estimation, is another manifestation of the Court Jews at work.

The fault line in the Jewish sensibility—however grand in its accomplishments and its many gifts to Western civilization eloquently recounted by Thomas Cahill in *The Gifts of the Jews*—is tectonic in its dimensions. Perhaps the single most resonant case study in self-division involves the institutional founder of the Christian faith. The story of St. Paul is too well known to require much in the way of comment, yet it is richly instructive. A rabid persecutor of the followers of Jesus, Saul of Tarsus experienced a blinding conversion to the new faith and was shortly thereafter called by the name of Paul (*Acts* 13:9). He then became the Apostle to the Gentiles, considering his Jewish identity a mere rehearsal for a larger identity and at times expressing strong disapproval of Jews who held to their traditional beliefs and identity. His quarrel with the Desposyni, the "servants of the Lord," led by James the brother of Jesus who wished to preserve the purity and exclusivity of the original faith, is a matter of scriptural record. In this respect, the Saul/Paul fracture represents a longstanding Jewish archetype.

This history of self-estrangement, political strife and cultural rupture has been played out from the biblical era through the centuries of religious factionalism and reciprocal excommunication culminating in our own epoch. The profound antipathy between assimilated Jews and their irredentist counterparts in Jerusalem, Tiberias, Safed and Hebron, as well as the caste-like contempt of Western Jewish intellectuals for the *Ostjuden*, that is, their assumed "plebeian" and "uneducated" East European brethren, are facts of modern Jewish history. The shame of many of the Jewish Councils in Nazi Europe that collaborated with their murderers (not all, as Gershom Scholem justifiably argues *in On Jews and Judaism in Crisis*) cannot be forgiven, despite attempts to explain it away as the least of worst alternatives.

The legacy of the celebrated Jewish philosopher Martin Buber and the equally acclaimed Jewish political writer Hannah Arendt, who could never forget their German patrimony and were corrosively suspicious of the Zionist project, has been broadly and unambiguously noxious. In the present moment we observe their offspring, that is, left-wing "peace activists," liberal rabbis, "post-Zionist" intellectuals, power nabobs, social ingratiators—in other words, Court Jews—who strive to erode the Jewish character of the state of Israel and so deprive it of its legitimacy. The Jewish Left, as it dances around the golden calf of a utopian project, represents perhaps the gravest danger to the survival of the country. Thus, they pursue their fugitive merit, ignoring the rain clouds until they are drenched and catch pneumonia, as the 19th century Jewish philosopher Max Nordau put it.

These are the "degraded" Jews whom the great Jewish patriot Vladimir Jabotinsky denounced. They are reminiscent of the spies that Moses sent out to reconnoiter enemy territory, ten of whom on returning compared themselves to frail grasshoppers before the fearsome Anakim and recoiled from their destiny (*Numbers* 13: 33). They do not understand, in the words of Nurit Greenger, that "Israel is the last station in the Jews' Via Dolorosa" and that "beyond this station is the Jews' final crucifixion," nor do they realize how profoundly they themselves are at risk. They have forgotten that the Jewish sense of security is always a false sense of security, that over the past 2000 years, as Melvin Konner points out in *Unsettled: An Anthropology of the Jews*, Jews have been expelled from 94 countries. They do not think to ask themselves why the future should be any different.

Renegade Jews especially have much to answer for. They are always happy to become token Jews, showcased at antisemitic seminars and congresses—where, as Alan Dershowitz writes in an article titled "Why Anti-Semitism Is Moving Toward the Mainstream," the "red lines separating legitimate criticism of Israel from subtle anti-Semitism" are now being crossed at will. These turncoats pose as principled anti-Zionists. In so being and doing, they acquire what historian Robert Wistrich calls "historic dissident status" by willfully providing their enemies with the ammunition they need to advance their cause while disguising their intentions. The syndrome has come to be known as Jew Flu.

Jews do not have the privilege enjoyed by all other peoples in the world, that is, the luxury of hating one another or, for that matter, of hating themselves. Other groups can get away with intramural conflict, the Islamic umma being the chief example of a community that can inflict enormous damage on itself, sundered between Sunni and Shia, nationalists and pan-Arabists, despotic regimes and the equally tyrannical Muslim Brotherhood. Due to its numbers, its domination of the United Nations, its vast oil reserves and its energy stranglehold on the rest of the planet, it survives robustly and continues to exercise global power. Jews have no such exemption.

A Jew who hates another Jew or who is mortified by his own Jewishness has given hostages to fortune and rendered his own prosperity and well-being, let alone his survival, hypothetical. The universal human prerogative of hating one's fellow man, whether members of one's race, ethnicity or nation, should be anathema to Jews since they of all peoples can least afford it. No less than Cain hated Abel or Jeroboam hated Rehoboam or Paul hated Saul, or radical progressivists hate Benjamin Netanyahu, the pathology continues to work its harm or, at the very least, to produce an etiology of dislocation in the self. One thinks of Israeli author Gilad Atzmon asserting in *The Wandering Who?* his "contempt for the Jew in me."

I fear that in our ceaseless squabbles and conflicts with one another, we may one day bring about our own demise. It is as if there is something in the Jewish soul that, despite its love of life, paradoxically hungers for its own extinction, as if the very quick of life, of practical wisdom, ethnic solidarity, love of the better part of heritage, faith in the political miracle known as Israel, and the stubborn desire to persist, will often lie dormant.

Under these circumstances, it is hard not to sympathize with the pungent and despairing remark of the Przysucha Hassidic Rebbe, Menachem Mendel of Kotzk, who said of his quarrelsome people: "I could revive the dead, but I have more difficulty reviving the living."

12
ISLAM'S WAR
ON THE PAST

We have heard much of the slash-and-burn frenzies of the Muslim hordes pillaging and slaughtering their way through parts of Africa and the Middle East. It is not only Christians, lapsed communicants, perceived heretics and foreigners who are the victims of their confessional ferocity and predatory aims, but the architecture and muniments of civilization itself. The threat which Islam poses to the life of the West should be obvious to anyone who is not complicit, gullible or mentally defective. To fully understand the menace, we must recognize that the Islamic attack is multi-pronged, taking place on a number of levels or fronts all working in concert, and gaining traction with every passing day.

Terror is the preferred means of those we call "extremists," "radicals," or (a new favorite) "gunmen," whether "lone wolves" (who often seem to roam in well-spaced packs) or established, heavily armed organizations the media like to refer to as "militants." The warrant for their habitual violence is rooted squarely in the *Koran* and the Hadith, not in poverty or unemployment despite assurances from their sympathizers and appeasers. As a Rand Corporation report on counterterrorism, cited by Raymond Ibrahim in a penetrating article for PJ Media, makes clear:

Terrorists are not particularly impoverished, uneducated, or afflicted by mental disease. Demographically, their most important characteristic is normalcy (within their environment). Terrorist leaders actually tend to come from relatively privileged backgrounds. Jihad, Ibrahim points out, "is integral to Islam, doctrinally and historically," located prominently within the founding scriptures and ancillary texts.

More potent in the long run than the tactic of terror is the strategy of massive immigration and refugee-ism, the poisoned fruit of multi-culturalism, enabling the metastasizing growth of Muslim populations in the progressively febrile democracies of the West. Once Islam in any of myriad forms is allowed into the body social, and in light of the agenda articulated in the Muslim Brotherhood's *An Explanatory Memorandum on the General Strategic Goal for the Group in North America*, a zymotic future is foreordained as societies begin to unravel and countries to lose their national character. Ten percent of the census is the tipping point. Scholars like Peter Hammond and the aforementioned Raymond Ibrahim have canvassed approximately 50 countries on four continents and done the math, and the results are indisputable.

The consequences of this covert invasion are glaringly evident in many European nations where Islamic no-go zones have proliferated, Sharia law has been incrementally introduced, thoroughfares have become prayer venues, welfare subsidies have been depleted, jihadist recruitment has escalated, rape has acquired the magnitude of a grooming epidemic (the true "rape culture"), and Muslim voting blocs can determine the outcome of elections, as conniving politicians are well aware. Such are the conditions that Western compromisers, accommodationists and tolerists, priding themselves on their putatively enlightened ideas, are ensuring for their progeny, if not for themselves.

Additionally, the Iranian march toward nuclear status is part of the Shi'ite plan for world domination, which in the Twelver version of the faith requires a universal conflagration and bloodletting to hasten or welcome the arrival of the Twelfth Imam, aka the Hidden Mahdi. The Middle East remains a tinderbox as civil wars erupt, nations fall apart, and Israel braces for the threat of nuclear attack. Iran and Saudi-Arabia have recently agreed to reestablish diplomatic ties, which bodes serious trouble for Israel, especially as Iran is reportedly fast approaching the nuclear threshold.

As we have been warned repeatedly by the most astute observers and critics among us—Robert Spencer, Steven Emerson, Andrew Bostom, Bruce Bawer, Raymond Ibrahim, Emmanuel Sivan, Serge Trifkovic, Geert Wilders, Peter Hammond, David Horowitz and others— we are under siege by the armies of a supremacist faith. To the array of hostile forces and tactics, we must add another front opened (or re-opened) by the warriors of Muhammad—*the offensive against the past.*

The Taliban demolition of the 1,700-year old Bamiyan Buddhas in 2001 and the near destruction of the ancient city of Palmyra should have sounded the alarm loud and clear. The systematic destruction of Hebrew/ Israeli artifacts attesting to the millennial sojourn of the Jewish people in the Holy Land, a project carried out by the Islamic *waqf* in control of the Temple Mount, is an undeniable attempt to erase the signs and proofs of the historical presence of an entire nation in what was always its natal homeland. Islamic militias rampage through the Middle East demolishing synagogues, churches, temples, palaces, statues, biblical tombs, historical monuments, remnant cities like Hatra and Nimrud, and inestimable cultural treasures anchoring antiquity to the living present.

What we are witnessing, working in tandem, as noted, with terror, social infiltration and the imminent nuclear and ballistic capability of a deranged and religiously dedicated rogue regime, is the deliberate and ongoing effacement of the historical, cultural and architectural record of Judeo-Christian civilization and its ancient precursors. The attack on ancient artifacts amounts to a surgical operation on the cultural psyche of the occident, a kind of *chronosectomy*, or removal of the temporal organ, leading ultimately to the gradual elimination of communal memory.

According to Daniel Pipes, the motive for this orgy of destruction is to "confirm the superior power of Muslims and, by implication, the truth of Islam." There is something to this, of course—a platitude need not be untrue. One will also agree with Robert Spencer's unexceptionable thesis that for the Muslim sensibility, the relics and shrines of "pre-Islamic civilizations, and non-Islamic civilizations, are all *jahiliyya*—the society of unbelievers, which is worthless," as stipulated in the *Koran* (3:137). But the real quarry is the historical logbook of the West and the material ledger of its antecedents. And the goal is their extirpation. This initiative against the collective memory of the West, tantamount to the razing of a world-historical library, is nothing less than an *auto-da-fé* of astronomical significance.

The barbaric iconoclasts of Islam have profited greatly from a tribe of elite Western academics. Looked at from the perspective of a mordant irony, it is as if the Islamic marauders constitute the activist arm of the Western university and its curricular reduction of the magisterial pageant of Western history in favor of a postmodern pastiche of marginal cultures, dubious movements and anti-Western polemics. The ground of desecration has been well prepared by a legion of witting and unwitting collaborators. This malignant tillage is now being pursued to its desired harvest, not only by an external enemy, but by a host of homegrown savages in the academy, the media and the political echelon.

The four-front assault—terror, social infiltration, nuclear arming and erasure of the past—is what the West is currently up against, but it remains plainly incapable of understanding or resisting the combined onslaught upon its cultural integrity, social consensus, political cohesion, and the traditional armature of its past, that is, the glue of retrocognition—Islam's renewed foray against the mind of the West. A person without memory is a hollow shell, living from moment to moment, unable to plan for the future or survive without help. A civilization that loses its heritage, whose evolutionary development is wiped out, and that no longer knows where it has come from or the identity of its parentage enjoys an aimless and frivolous existence until it eventually collapses and disappears. It survives paradoxically only in the triumphant if sketchy memory of the civilization that has replaced it. The eclipse of memory, the decoupling of the archive from the present, is nothing short of death by other means. When, owing to the eradication of memory, time no longer functions as a sustaining medium, the will to persist is paralyzed and life becomes meaningless. The murder of the past is a particularly effective form of cultural homicide.

The long march through the institutions is growing shorter by the day.

13

THE MAP OF LOVE
AND MISREADING

The Anglo-Egyptian novelist Ahdaf Soueif is not a bad writer but she's not a very good one either. Her reputation rests mainly on one book, *The Map of Love*, which sold over a million copies and was shortlisted for the 1999 Man Booker Prize, and on some tendentious and partisan political journalism for *The Guardian*. What unites her fiction and her journalism is an overt sympathy for the Palestinians—she was the founder of the annual Palestine Festival of Literature—and a corresponding hostility toward Israel. Clearly, these are political attitudes that endear her to a literary establishment and wide readership who share these conventional left-wing and pro-Islamic sentiments, and which may partially account for the book's success.

Publishers Weekly anoints Soueif as "the intellectual heir of Edward Said," and there is certainly a modicum of truth to this promotion to the ranks of influence and repute. In her slanted and one-sided *Guardian* essay, "Under the Gun," collected in Mezzaterra: Fragments from the Common Ground, she laments that her life "has been overcast by the shadow of Israel," proceeds to reduce the complex nature of Israeli-Palestinian relations to the dimensions of a fairy tale, misrepresents UN Resolution 242 in passing, and raises the 2000 Intifada to the heights of an epic struggle of the pristinely innocent against the barbarously guilty. For Soueif, "the discord between the Arab world and the U.S. is entirely to do with Israel," aping the palpably flawed position associated with Said and his followers, like John Mearsheimer and Stephen Walt in their shabbily confected *The Israel Lobby*. Soueif does her best to advance and popularize such gross distortions of truth in both her commentary and her fiction.

The Map of Love pushes all the right buttons in the great console of ready-made opinion that prevails today. It purports to be a love story unfolding on several parallel historical planes, set a century apart in colonial and modern Egypt. An English widow, Anne Winterbourne, moves to Egypt and falls in love with an irredentist radical, Sharif Pasha al-Baroudi, whom she marries in 1901. In 1997, her great granddaughter, Isabel Parkman, embarks from New York on a journey to Egypt to trace her family history, and falls in love with the symphony conductor and activist Omar al-Ghamrawi who has embraced the Palestinian cause, an obvious surrogate for Edward Said.

The novel is admittedly rich in evocative description but is fatally weakened by an air of romantic sensationalism, an *haut goût* of maudlin evangelism and an insinuating current of predictable disinformation.

Soueif's novel brings to mind another cartographical production, Harold Bloom's celebrated critical volume, *A Map of Misreading* (a companion to *The Anxiety of Influence*). Among the various litcrit categories or "revisionary ratios" that Bloom develops we find one he names "Apophrades" (from the Greek for "impure days," inauspicious events"), which he redefines as a form of poetic and literary influence resembling "the Return of the Dead"—the great writers of the past who haunt and intimidate the present-day author with precisely their greatness. What Bloom calls "the imagination's struggle with its own origins" leads to the imagination surrendering to a "teleological error," its projected ends marred by a faulty and melodramatic reading of both its past and its present.

In the case of *The Map of Love*, the structure of this device is repeated on the plane of narrative. The writer constructs a false tableau of the *now* that is meant to subsume and transcend the sentimental ideal of the *then*. It is, in effect, an impure or inauspicious transaction. A supposedly exalted past when men were heroic and larger than life and women were wise and adventurous is reprised and strengthened in a simulating present.

Within the tissue of the narrative, Omar is clearly a

contemporary update of the exotic, fearless, and tribally dedicated Sharif, as if Soueif were enacting a parody of the primal scene of Freudian repetition, or in Bloom's terminology, as if she had invested in "the compulsion to repeat the precursor's patterns" in an attempt "to recover the prestige of origins...since such mediation holds open the perpetual possibility of one's own sublimity." Omar's sublimity, however, is not persuasive; it is simply posited by authorial fiat. Indeed, Soueif's stock in trade seems to be a manufactured glamor painted onto wooden characters.

But beyond the boundaries of the novel, as we have noted, Omar is intended to suggest Edward Said. He represents Soueif's deceptive and largely untenable effort to valorize a literary and cultural giant who is now coming increasingly to look like the petty, hypocritical and mendacious doyen of a generation of leftwing postmodern intellectuals. *The Map of Love* is, finally, little more than a pulpy yet insidious piece of Islamic and Palestinian special pleading and a sorry attempt to rescue the endangered reputation of a morally tainted and intellectually dishonest scholar.

I wish to avoid Bloomian technicalities. Simply put, apophrades is the mode of thought which brings a dominant, commanding and *idealized* past into the given moment in order to create an even greater and more ennobled present. This imaginary time-transfer, Bloom warns, creates a present which subsequently vanishes between the two antithetical poles of the "past-in-the-future" (e.g., a projected restored Caliphate) and "the future-in-the-past" (e.g., a wished-for 7th century revival), which is exactly the historical dilemma of contemporary Islam and, *mutatis mutandis*, of the Palestinian dream world. The Palestinian *nomenklatura* presupposes an ancient people and an idealized nation that never existed but which is taken as a past reality. This bogus construct is then elevated into a conceptual present which promises to be a restoration, a fulfillment and, ultimately, an even grander and more resilient political fact. But the possible and *sustainable* present—a viable, democratic and prosperous sovereign state living in peace with its neighbor—is lost in the gap between an apocryphal memory and a spurious future.

In *The Map of Love*, Ahdaf Soueif is playing the apophradic game, conjuring the Return of the Dead—or the Return of the Illusory—to affront the living with impossibility. On one level a literary artifact, it is on another, deeper level a subliminal political manifesto. She establishes an equation or "revisionary ratio" between 19th century England and Egypt on the one hand and modern Israel and "Palestine" on the other, all the while touting Edward Said as the visionary leader and prophet who labors for a desired future. As Egypt eventually triumphed in its quest for independence at the expense of imperial Britain, so "Palestine" will presumably realize its successful struggle against Israeli oppression, as Said urged and assumed in *The Question of Palestine* and other books.

That the equation is invalid, that the Palestinians never constituted a coherent and hereditary people, that their past and their future have no common boundary in a feasible or workable present, and that Israel, according to international law, the laws of war and facts on the ground, is not an occupying power—all this has no purchase on what is essentially, to cite Bloom again, a phony substitution of "early for late and late for early."

Meanwhile, Soueif has done her tawdry and clandestine job, to nobody's advantage except perhaps her own and those who gain from pushing the Palestinian fable. The map of love is really a map of misreading. A false prophet is given messianic credibility and the possibility of a productive present falls between the antipodes of a corrupted past and an anterior future.

14

ISLAMOPEPSY:
A NEW PATHOLOGY

In a YouTube symposium of world-class scholars and political authors, Paul Williams, Melanie Phillips, Bernard Lewis and Mark Steyn united to articulate a grim and pressing warning to a seemingly insensible Western world. As Steyn tells it, the world's most advanced societies are starting to go out of business, on the one hand refusing to assess and confront the gathering Islamic storm that threatens their survival and, on the other, losing out in the reproductive sweepstakes. Europe in particular is poised to suffer a Damoclean fate. Tracing an inverted family tree in which four grandparents and two parents produce one child, the continent is losing the battle of generational replenishment. It is only a matter of time before Europe as we know it closes shop and a burgeoning Islamic *ummah* accomplishes its version of an unfriendly corporate takeover.

Meanwhile, it would be a mistake to conclude that a

vibrant and rejuvenated Islam is patiently waiting for the inevitable historical denouement to occur. On the contrary, even as it prepares to celebrate its demographic triumph, it is robustly—and successfully—pursuing its evident intention to assert itself as a destabilizing factor in European society. And its most powerful ally in its campaign of eventual conquest is the European postmodern elite itself, for whom one truth is as good as another and no culture is worse than any other—with the exception, naturally, of the Judeo-Christian armature of norms and values now regarded as both passé and expendable. Europe's political class, public intellectuals, journalists, activist judges, talking heads and, oddly enough, parts of the clergy—Pope Francis is a resonant example—have banded together as a fifth column to usher in a new dispensation, which Bat Ye'or and others have aptly dubbed Eurabia.

How could so unprecedented a collapse of will and principle have taken place? How is it possible that, in the words of Bernard Lewis from the video discussion, Muslims "now consider Europe the House of Islam"? And that the European intelligentsia have given them the key to the front door?

The continent is suffering from what we might call *Islamolepsy*, the kind of rigidity found in schizophrenia and hypnotic trances, now transposed upon a collective cultural sensibility and reducing it to a condition of social and political helplessness. It does not know how to fight back; indeed, apart from a few pitiful twitches like banning articles of clothing or uttering proclamations of intent, it is increasingly incapable of doing so. *Shari'a* law is gradually being introduced in Britain, a harbinger of things to come in other EU countries. Counter episodes are unconvincing. Much has been made, for example, of Switzerland's curtailing of minarets, but the new mega-mosque in Cologne, Germany, will boast two 18-storey high minarets, and in Belgium Christian churches are being turned into mosques, a scene straight out of French novelist Jean Raspail's premonitory *The Camp of the Saints*. There are currently 6000 mosques in Europe and the number is growing.

Far more worrisome, America as well may be gradually succumbing to the same pandemic. Melanie Phillips, author of *Londonistan* and *The World Turned Upside Down*, laments that Europe now malingers in a state of denial, "and to a certain extent, America too." The major concern is whether or not Islam should be permitted to infiltrate the living plasm of American society.

What is most astonishing is that the question even needs to be raised *in the first place*, since the slightest acquaintance with the historical brunt of Islam, its desire to establish a world-dominant Caliphate, its 1400-year record of conquest, spoliation and oppression, its doctrinal ordnance which enjoins the suppression or murder of the infidel in *surah* after *surah* of the *Koran* and the ancillary literature, its practice of *taqiyya* (or obligatory lying as a form of defense under duress, as in *Koran* 16: 106, which has been interpreted to mean deception in order to promote its underlying agenda) and its campaign to impose *shari'a* law upon the social and juridical framework of a free society—all this should have alerted us immediately to the menace. That is, assuming we are awake and sentient.

The sort of contentions we have been witnessing could only occur in favored societies—the U.S. no less than Europe—for which the real world lies somewhere beyond their borders, despite the blows they may have received. As a result, they can preoccupy themselves with febrile pieties, idle or inexpedient disputes, recondite theories, sentimental indulgences, intellectual fantasies and utopian schemes that must inevitably fail. These are societies that are able to preen themselves on their sophistication and enlightenment only because they have managed to retire into an arbor of relative peace and considerable opulence. They feel no hazard in inviting the 7th century into the 21st while deprecating their own traditions, usages and foundational premises. It should be conceded, however, that the chief culprits in the charade of self-delegitimation derive mainly from the more advantaged and connected strata of society.

None of these influential appeasers seems to understand what is going on out there beyond their insulated thought bubbles—though some, it may be, only pretend not to. And none seems to be at all disconcerted by the far more serious problem to which Michael Ledeen drew our attention, the 1200 radical mosques that stipple the American landscape, breeding grounds for the Islamization of the United States.

The propitiators among us are equally blind to an attendant and escalating phenomenon, namely, jihadi training camps like Islamberg in upstate New York where recruits and converts to the Faith Militant are taught to handle firearms and acquire bomb-making skills. As Paul Williams, author of *The Day of Islam*, disclosed, Islamberg is only one of thirty such compounds across the U.S., affiliated with Jamat al-Fuqra, a paramilitary organization founded by Pakistani cleric Sheik Mubarak Ali Gilani. These are Waziristan-type enclaves on American soil which are being allowed to ramify and which have already committed acts of violence, including firebombings and assassinations going back to the 1980s. And yet little is being done to police or dismantle them.

Perhaps the most distressing fact of all is not so much the craftiness of the Muslim actors in the current drama—this is to be expected—but the utter naivety and mental sclerosis of our media mavens, public intellectuals and a hefty segment of the political class who have rallied to the Islamic cause—though perhaps this too was to be expected. The "willful blindness" that Andrew McCarthy speaks about, and explores more fully in *The Grand Jihad: How Islam and the Left Sabotage America*, has descended upon us like a biblical plague, which is now beginning to look like a permanent condition. A toxic mix of credulousness and fear has infected an entire generation of ingenues, sophists, socialist fellow-travelers, timeservers and sycophants who are devotedly bringing their country into harm's way. How can we explain what is nothing less than a passion for self-immolation, a welcoming of the encroaching darkness?

What we are observing, I suspect, is the onset of a debilitating disorder which manifests as a seizure of the mental organ, a lack of elasticity in responding to complex and threatening situations. It is as if the mind has been paralyzed by a variant form of cataleptic fit, characterized by fixity of posture, obliviousness to external stimuli, loss of control and diminished sensitivity to pain. The malady is induced by profound emotional shock accompanied by withdrawal from reality—an unconscious way, perhaps, of amortizing the great multicultural blunder for which we are responsible but cannot admit to ourselves. Knowing subliminally that we have been instrumental in soliciting our own ruin, and too weak to respond decisively, the only asylum that remains is a species of dementia that shields us from the truth.

In other words, those who suffer from the distemper, as it emerges in the social and political sphere, are simply unable to acknowledge, absorb and confront the magnitude of what is transpiring before their very eyes. They cannot discriminate among the external stimuli or recognize them for what they are. Suicide bombings, terrorist strikes, multiple casualties, stealth jihad, meretricious vouchers of good intentions, legal assaults, cultural implosion, a billion and a half-strong adversary riding the wave of the future—it is all too much for our Islamoleptic media, intelligentsia, entertainers and political masters to fully take in. It appears they have sought refuge from the unassimilable in a classic fugue state or succumbed to split-mind syndrome. As Martin Amis astutely comments in *The Second Plane*, "The death cult always benefits, initially at least, from its capacity to astonish and stupefy." I quibble only with Amis' "initially." The trouble is that once stupefaction sets in, it tends to make itself at home.

The etiology of the affliction that merits the name of Islamolepsy issues, it bears repeating, in a host of predictable symptoms: the rejection of personal complicity, the denial of palpable reality, the construction of an alternate world in which a bellicose and inimical claim to ascendancy is blithely endorsed, the rigid and untenable conviction of superior insight, the false consolation of intellectual torpor and, of course, the tendency to fall back on moral histrionics to discredit those who can still see clearly.

The prognosis is not encouraging, for Islamolepsy

resembles the most tenacious and virulent of pathologies. Perhaps it is even incurable.

15

THE ENIGMA OF
JEWISH IDENTITY

Like many Jews of a largely secular persuasion, or like those who oscillate between doubt and belief, I have often wondered what I had to do with other "flavors" of Jewish communicants. Strolling along the streets of Montreal's Outremont borough, home to a substantial Orthodox society, I feel absolutely no connection to the black-coated, earlocked, fur-hatted inhabitants who hasten by me without so much as a glance, immured in their own sequestered worlds. They may be bent on the preservation of Halachic Judaism and the maintenance of a sacramental community, but they have little interest in the world beyond their exclusionary domain and certainly none in the lives of individuals like me. "Ghetto orthodoxy," writes James Parkes in *A History of the Jewish People*, "has no understanding of the moral problems of a modern and independent state." Or, he might have continued, of modern and independent people.

Similarly, encountering Reformist and Reconstructionist Jews at local events, I feel no affinity with such nominal adherents to a faith they have re-interpreted as little more than a cultural tradition, that is, a set of mores and usages without serious reference to the God of the Hebrew scripture, the Mosaic and Noahide commandments, the principles of *Halakhic* law, the poetry of David and Solomon, or the magnificent fulminations of the great prophets. How would they respond if angels appeared at their doors, as before Abraham (*Genesis* 18), or a divine command resonated in their ears, as in the *Book of Jeremiah* and the *Book of Jonah*, or a latter-day Elijah descended upon their complacency? Heaven forfend!

Between these two constellations of Jewish postulants, the ersatz and the genuine, the gap appears unbridgeable. In what way can they be regarded as members of the same extended family? Observing common holidays to which Jews attribute different meanings on a scale of spiritual gravity is not a binding agent but merely a fugitive exercise in consanguinity. I am reminded of a Jewish joke that underlines the problem. An Orthodox and a Reform rabbi find themselves seated side by side at a religious conference. In the process of getting to know one another, the Orthodox rabbi recounts that he has recently officiated at a Bar Mitzvah in which he was informed that the celebrant received the gift of a Harley. Puzzled, he asks his Reform neighbor, "But what is a

Harley?" "It's a motorcycle," comes the reply, "but what's a Bar Mitzvah?"

And then, of course, there is the mob of Jewish an-tisemites and anti-Zionists (which amounts pretty well to the same thing these days) whose names swell the roll-call of Judaism's treacherous sons and daughters—a prime example of how a historical community can attack itself like an immune system gone haywire. The prophet Isaiah correctly foretold the future: "Thy destroyers ... shall go forth of thee" (49:17). The so-called Jewish S.H.I.T. list (Self-Hating and/or Israel-Threatening Jews) furnishes the names of nearly 8000 contemporary Jewish tergiver-sators. These are people who casually court disaster in the remorseless anti-Jewish and anti-Zionist posture they af-fect, aiming their execrations and weaponizing their prose against their fellows. Living in what I've elsewhere called a latter-day Iberian delusion—if one recalls the eventual fate of the Spanish *conversos*—their only consolation in the ever-possible event of a resurgent and maniacal anti-Jew-ish national movement is that, like the Jewish Councils in Nazi Europe, they would be among the last to go, once their revisionist services were no longer needed by the demons they have agreed to traffic with.

What is it, then, that ultimately brings us together, that presumably unifies us as a people, and that, in effect, paints the bulls-eye on our backs? The answer should be obvious: it is precisely that which sews the yellow badge upon our lapels. As the great Zionist visionary Theodor Herzl came to believe, the Jew is defined by his enemies. However else he may understand himself, a Jew is also a Jew by default, in the same way that Hans Meyer (a.k.a. Jean Améry), as he recounts in *At The Mind's Limits*, discovered he was a Jew with the passing of the Nuremburg Laws in 1935. A Jew remains a Jew even without positive determinants.

What many Jews do not seem to understand about antisemitism is that it is both a ubiquitous and an equal-opportunity pathology. As former Canadian Minister of Justice Irwin Cotler said at the signing of the Ottawa Protocol, a welcome if belated attempt to codify and affirm resistance to this malignant phenomenon, antisemitism is not only the longest known form of hatred in the history of humanity, it is the only form of hatred that is truly global. However we may describe it—as an irrational revulsion, or the need to scapegoat a convenient group for supposedly inexplicable miseries and reverses of which that group is innocent, or classic projection, or, to cite Ruth Wisse writing in *The Weekly Standard*, "the organization of politics against the Jews" in order to "win rather than assume the allegiance of subjects or citizens" —it eventually strikes Jews everywhere and indiscriminately. For the antisemite, all Jews are alike regardless of their politics, their professions, the degrees of their faith or lack of such, or even their rebellious and venomous denunciations of their own brethren.

There is a passage in Amos Oz's *A Tale of Love and Darkness* that makes this collapsing of distinctions painfully clear. Referring to the Nazi "cleansing operations" in the Polish town of Rovno, he writes: "the Germans opened fire and slaughtered on the edge of pits, in two days, some twenty-five thousand souls … well-to-do and proletarian, pious, assimilated, and baptized, communal leaders, synagogue functionaries, peddlers and drawers of water, Communists and Zionists, intellectuals, artists, and village idiots, and some four thousand babies."

The message is that we're all incriminated. As I wrote in *The Big Lie*, "Warm Jews, lukewarm Jews and cold Jews are equally at risk. At the end of the day, the antisemite never stopped to take their temperature." Similarly, as the *Jerusalem Post* commented after the Mumbai massacre in November 2008 in which Chabad House was attacked and its occupants murdered, "the terrorists did not inquire whether their victims were haredi, Orthodox, traditional or secular." If Noam Chomsky or Jennifer Lowenstein had happened to be on the premises, they, too, would have been tortured and killed. In the minds of Jew-haters, being Jewish is sufficient warrant to disqualify a person from remaining a member of the human race.

It is this perennial hatred, I submit, that forms the peculiar ethnic or historical collagen that binds the Jew to his community, even should he repudiate his people with his whole soul or turn against them with the rancor of the benighted. This vicious odium is the force or substance that constitutes his or her identity. Jewishness obviously has nothing to do with race, as the Nazis believed, since there are Jews of every hue and physical type. To define a Jew according to rabbinic law as someone born to a Jewish mother only begs the question and involves us in a *regressus*—what makes a Jewish mother Jewish, apart from excessive nagging and the artful manipulation of guilt? Is Jewish identity a function of following the thirteen articles of faith articulated by Maimonides? But not all Jews are capable of abiding by every one of these, and the last article asserting belief in the resurrection of the dead is hardly substantiated in the Old Testament, in which there are, depending on how one counts, only six references to the afterlife. Rabbi Akiva proposed that knowledge of the Torah is the essential touchstone of Jewishness, in which case the majority of the world's Jews are not really Jewish at all and a certain number of Gentiles are.

Here and there a rare and tenuous bloodline may connect a given individual to incorrigible Habiru ancestors even the patriarchs and the prophets despaired of ever civilizing. They cannot be more than a handful and must remain undetectable. And it is far from clear whether even these originals may be considered "Jews," a designation which came appreciably later. As the *Koran* rightly suggests, neither Abraham nor Moses were Jews; it appears that Mordecai of the *Book of Esther* was the first to be called a Jew.

Jean-Paul Sartre in *Anti-Semite and Jew: An Exploration of the Etiology of Hate* may not have been far off the mark when he said "a Jew is someone who is called a Jew" and "it is the anti-semite who creates the Jew." This may not be the whole story but, counter-intuitive or even flippant as it may sound to some, it is an important chapter— perhaps *the* most important chapter. Jews who happen to have escaped the stigma are either exceedingly fortunate or blindly oblivious.

Jews should take their cue from the Muslim Brotherhood, especially the electoral program of its Egyptian parent. The crowd assembled at the Al-Azhar mosque in Cairo chant: "one day we shall kill all the Jews." Their primary quarry is Israel, of course, but Jews in the Diaspora are also targeted for extinction. As Joseph Klein writes, "The rally was co-sponsored by the Al-Azhar University, which President Obama had referred to as a 'beacon of learning.'" But this presumptive beacon has diffused its excoriating light not only through the Middle East; it has sent its leprous influence into the chanceries and public squares of the non-Muslim West as well. Much of Europe has already become a danger zone for Jews. Acts of anti-Jewish vandalism and instances of hostility to the Jewish state and its supporters are clearly on the rise in America. And both the European and American governments are conspicuously sympathetic to the Brotherhood, whose gradual ascendance to power they have facilitated.

The Brotherhood of hatred, however, is plainly not only Muslim in origin. It is a Brotherhood with a lengthy past in the blood-soaked abattoirs of Europe and also in the realm of public and official sentiment in North America, in particular among the camarilla of the Left—which is, rather perversely, the home of a plurality of Jewish voters as well. Nonetheless, the meeting of poisoned minds grows more intimate by the day—a confluence that makes little distinction between the diverse forms of Judaism, including its secular and revisionist varieties.

Some Jews may drive BMWs, but their near ancestors were transported in cattle cars. Some Jews live in decent or luxurious houses, but their relatives were brutalized in the *mellah*. Some Jews may pride themselves on their elegance and sophistication, but they remain apes and pigs for the Muslim world. Others believe that political calculation will work to their advantage. One remembers Rabbi Stephen Wise, Co-Chair of the American Zionist Emergency Council during World War II, who downplayed the horror of the Holocaust and even obstructed relief efforts in order, according to his lights, not to vex or offend the Roosevelt administration. Such reasoning would not have cut much ice with the millions who died in the Shoah or its survivors.

As Matthew Hausman points out in his seminal essay,

"Secular Idolatry in American Jewish Leadership" many Jewish organizations in the U.S., such as the Anti-Defamation League and the Jewish Theological Seminary, as well as many secular Jewish leaders, "have been addled by their slavish devotion to an ideological agenda that in the name of tolerance has excused hateful rhetoric masquerading as political discourse—particularly when that rhetoric comes from the Left." Their disposition "to deny their history, or to accept as fact the national and religious myths of those who wish to subjugate and destroy them," reveals that they are simply a more nebulous version of *nominal* Jews. Hausman concludes, rightly: "Community leaders lose all credibility when they advocate or excuse policies that compromise the safety of Israel or threaten Jewish survival." Such leaders are the tactical connivers among the Jewish public who elevate a political or electoral priority above whatever might be said to constitute the corpus of Jewish values. They, too, in any worst-case scenario, would go the way of their fellows.

Others still are convinced that assimilation or recreancy has served to render them impervious to the black winds of history, but political weather is unpredictable and they may yet find themselves facing the blast. As for a significant portion of the Jewish cognitive class, their credentials are no antidote to intellectual seizure and no remedy for the discomfiture or reprisals they may one day be made to feel. The antisemite is not impressed by probity, achievement, like-mindedness, secularity or the inevitable social and professional disparities. Differences tend to be scrubbed out, for the truth is that Jews remain Jews by negative definition, despite claims to the contrary or the assertion of some mysterious entelechy that accounts for their chronicled essence.

There are some things that cannot be evaded. Mortality is one. Antisemitism is another. And the Jew is subject to both. The former establishes his common humanity. But the latter fixes his decisive and unappealable identity.

16

THE LIES OF
GÜNTER GRASS

It's a curious fact that the reputation of many contemporary novelists of popular distinction rests on a single book. Think, for example, of Umberto Eco. Had he not written *The Name of the Rose*, he would be better known today as an essayist and semiotician who had also published some interesting if not particularly memorable fiction. (The one exception to the rule might be his *Foucault's Pendulum*.) This is even truer of Norwegian antisemite, Jostein Gaarder, whose *Sophie's World* catapulted him to international acclaim. The works that followed might best be portrayed as competent-to-forgettable. Ditto the anti-Zionist Louis De Bernière whose *Captain Corelli's Mandolin* was his one resonant success, and Portuguese antisemite and Nobel Laureate José Saramago, whose only readable book was *The Year of the Death of Ricardo Reis*.

As for Germany's most famous contemporary novelist, Günter Grass pretty well consorts with the paradigm, *The Tin Drum* having established him as a major figure in the rolls of literary mavenry. Admittedly, subsequent books like *Dog Years* and *The Flounder* were notable achievements. But absent the beating of *The Tin Drum*, the callithumpian parade of Grass' works in the public arena would have been far less spectacular. He cannot be dismissed as a one-shot Johnny, but his oeuvre arguably does not justify his inflated réclame. Indeed, for some time, he lived off the interest from the capital he invested in his heyday.

This did not prevent him from generating considerable controversy with the publication in the German daily *Süddeutschen Zeitung* of an anti-Israeli poem titled *What Must Be Said* (*Was gesagt werden muss*). As Sebastian Hammelehle informs us in *Der Spiegal Online*, the German expression "what must be said" connotes the conversational cliché "There's no law against saying that ... " which would appear to carry the same smarmy patina in our culture as "Some of my best friends are Jews." Grass did not hesitate to assert in the poem that Israel is a country "to which I am bound." The lie is so palpable as to be embarrassing.

Similarly, Frank Schirrmacher, an editor at the Frankfurter *Allgemeine Zeitung*, points out that Grass' use of the word *Überlebende* (survivor) "to describe his situation and the plight of Germans in the event of an Israeli attack on Iran," is disingenuous. "Traditionally, the word 'survivor' is associated—in a German-language context—with Jewish survivors of the Shoah." Schirrmacher believes that Grass, who in his youth was a member of the Nazi Waffen SS, was engaged in a duplicitous attempt to "make peace with his own biography."

It must be said that, whatever his motives and talents may have been, Grass is obviously not a poet and *What Must Be Said* is demonstrably not a poem. The language of the piece is scarcely even workmanlike, fishtailing between the unctuously pulpiteering and the colorlessly prosaic. There is nothing about this dismal effort that says "I have to be a poem." Had it been written as a short prose essay with a heavily propagandistic slant, there would have been no detectable difference. The thing has no literary merit whatsoever; to put it bluntly, it is an execrable piece of fustian.

The same can be said of the sentiment the "poem" expresses, which, as Hammelehle puts it, constitutes a "lyrical first strike" against the Jewish state. Except that there is nothing lyrical about a flat and pompous verbal eructation riddled with lies, false assumptions, evasions and catarrhal flecks of disinformation.

When Grass opposed the sale to Israel of a German submarine "whose specialty consists of guiding all-destroying warheads to where the existence/Of a single atomic bomb is unproven," he was indulging once again in a species of mendacity. The clear implication was that Israel contemplated a nuclear first-strike against Iran, which is as far from the truth as the canard that the Holocaust never happened. Israel may have been contemplating a pre-emptive *conventional* attack on Iran's nuclear facilities, but Israel's nuclear arsenal is geared to second-strike retaliation. And regarding Grass' contention that the existence of an Iranian atomic bomb was "unproven," the circumstantial evidence that the mullahs are amassing a thermonuclear potential is overwhelming.

Further, when Grass argued that "the nuclear power of Israel endangers/The already fragile world peace," he was so profoundly divorced from reality as to render him clinically *non compos*. It is the nuclear power of rogue states like North Korea and Pakistan that endangers world peace, pathological entities governed by unstable ruling councils in thrall to incendiary ideologies that threaten us all. And, barring intervention, they are soon to be joined by a radical Shi'ite state committed to nothing short of hegemonic violence.

Defaming Israel as a "perpetrator" of "recognized danger" and urging it to "renounce violence," when such admonitions would properly apply to the Palestinians, Hezbollah and Iran, placed Grass squarely in the camp of the lunatic Left—where, in fact, he had been malingering for much of his activist career. And when he affirmed that he could not be silent because he was "tired of the hypocrisy of the West," he revealed himself as not only ignorant and self-infatuated, but as a prime example of the hypocrisy he liked to denounce. For the brief that he mounted in his poem mirrors almost precisely the conduct of the West vis à vis the Jewish state. There is precious little sunlight between them.

One might have felt sorry for Günter Grass had he not been so dangerous, exploiting his reputation—even if based on one undoubted success—to foster a deception that encourages the enemy who schemes not only Israel's, but our demise as well. It is no surprise that former Iranian Deputy Culture Minister Javad Shamaqdiri eulogized Grass' poem as a "literary work of human and historical responsibility [that] warns beautifully." What should be said is that Günter Grass was a pitiable specimen of bad faith and muddled thinking who sounded current, given that he parroted the Leftist line. His legacy, however, is much diminished. From the perspective of his actual writing and reputation, the Grass was greener in the distant past; today, to quote a genuine poet, John Keats, it is a withered sedge where "no birds sing."

17

THE CITY OF
SLAUGHTER

In 1903, the Jewish community in the town of
Kishinev, the capital of the Russian province of
Bessarabia, was decimated by a pogrom, a frequent
occurrence in that part of the world. It was triggered by
the age-old blood libel, the Jewish inhabitants of the town
suspected of murdering a young Christian boy and using
his blood in the baking of matzo. The riot lasted three
days, killing and wounding hundreds of Jews, destroying
houses and looting businesses. As the *New York Times* for
April 28, 1903 reported, "At sunset the streets were piled
with corpses and wounded. Those who could make their
escape fled in terror, and the city is now practically desert-
ed of Jews."

Events of this barbarous nature have been a commonplace of Jewish history, whether in Eastern and Central Europe or in the Holy Land, whether in Kishinev or
in Hebron where 67 Jewish men, women and children

were butchered and the Jewish community expelled in the anti-Jewish riots of 1929. These are only two of the more notable "incidents" in an uninterrupted chronicle of antisemitic bloodletting, culminating in the Holocaust and morphing today into the multipronged attack by the Muslim world, the international left, the United Nations and European capitals on the Jewish state.

The rampage in Kishinev, however, has assumed a kind of emblematic status owing to a celebrated poem, "The City of Slaughter," by Israel's national laureate, Chaim Nachman Bialik, who visited the town to prepare a report on the massacre. Few read the report today but the poem, over 400 lines long and filled with macabre detail and vehement denunciation, has become part of the Jewish archive, and is said to have contributed to strengthening the Zionist project and to the eventual formation of the paramilitary Hagannah in Mandate Palestine. Interested readers might be moved to consult Simon Dubnow's *History of the Jews in Russia and Poland* and the essay collection *Pogroms: Anti-Jewish Violence in Modern Russian History*.

What makes the poem especially memorable is not only its vivid account of the pogrom but its undisguised condemnation of Jewish passivity and abject resignation—in some instances, as we know, even of collaboration—in the face of endemic Jew-hatred and the repeated eruptions of carnage to which Jewish communities were subjected. Its description of Jewish men cowering in cel-

lars while their women were being raped and disembow-
eled is utterly harrowing and unforgettable. Bialik knew,
as Daniel Gordis explains in a seminal essay, *"The Shame
of It All,"* that the re-creation of Israel was "about changing the condition of the Jew, by changing the nature of
the Jew."

Jews could no longer sit back, defenseless and afraid,
while their people were being terrorized and killed. A
state would need to be re-established in which the Jewish people would refuse to be the helpless victims of the
world's undying enmity, "shocked by what is done to them
[and] infuriated by their powerlessness," as Gordis writes.
And so, in the course of time it came to pass that Israel rose again from the darkness of history, not without
great suffering and continued slaughter, but with pride,
conviction, strength and purpose. Bialik's poem, with its
unsparing judgment of Jewish docility and nonresistance,
was instrumental in "changing the nature of the Jew."

Not entirely however. For among the Jewish population both in Israel and in the Diaspora are many who,
like their Kishinev forebears, remain feeble and compliant, timorous conciliators rather than courageous fighters.
They live in modern cities, not in *shtetls* and ghettos. Most
flaunt university and college degrees, not yeshiva parch-
ment, and preen themselves on their sophistication and
putative insights. The texts they bend over, indifferent to
the fury that rages around them, are not the sacred scrolls

of the faith, as was the case with their ancestors, but trea-
tises of propitiation, anti-Zionist screeds and manifestos
of spurious enlightenment. The result is, *mutatis mutandis*,
the same. True, they no longer cower in cellars while their
women are being defiled, but their complicity in the campaign to weaken the Jewish state, reduce its borders to indefensible proportions and encourage its adversaries who
wish to destroy it, is evident. They are content to watch
Israel being raped and dismembered.

Indeed, many actually facilitate the process. Elhanan
Yakira in his important 2010 book, *Post-Zionism, Post-Ho-
locaust*, transfers Bialik's thesis into the contemporary milieu, speaking passionately about "the participation of
Jews and Israelis in the anti-Zionist campaign," which he
regards as "in effect ... annihilationist," as a position characterized by "ignorance, bad faith, or malice" adopted by
a "community of opprobrium." It is nothing short of a
"moral disaster" perpetrated by the descendants of Bialik's colony of submissives who today have transformed
the acceptance of victimhood into the disparagement of
their own.

For the Court Jews are everywhere, the kapos
abound, the so-called "peace" constituency retains its
prominence, left wing Jewish professors work tirelessly in
classrooms, lecture halls, blogs, articles and op-eds to delegitimize an embattled nation, rabbinical fellow-travelers
engage in "dialogue" with antisemites and support influ-

ential figures ill-disposed toward the Jewish state, Jewish voting blocs mobilize on behalf of their antagonists and betrayers, Israeli revisionist historians and Jewish UN apparatchiks act as Palestinian water-carriers, Jewish public intellectuals and journalists propose solutions to the Middle East conflict that would lead to the disappearance of Israel, directors of Jewish organizations invite Palestinian jihadists to lecture them, or abet sanctions against Israel, or back a unilateral declaration of Palestinian statehood. These trimmers and delinquents stubbornly deny who their real enemies are, as they saunter cheerfully toward the abattoir. For those who want names and addresses, I provide a compendious list of such tergiversators in *Hear, O Israel!*. But the most reprehensible among them are already well known.

Bialek still has their measure. This is why his poem stays fresh and contemporary and needs to be read not simply as a literary artifact but as a political lesson for the present and a warning for the future. I present below a sort of hybrid version, a cross between an adaptation and a free translation, substantially abridged and focusing on the spiritual and intellectual defection of far too many Jews wherever they may be found. I have taken a few small liberties in the rendering but I believe they are warranted in the evolving context of cultural resilement among a significant element of modern Jewry. The message of the poem is no less relevant today, when the very existence of Israel is increasingly threatened and terrorist charters call for the killing of Jews, than it was in 1903 when the Zionist movement was just gaining momentum.

From *The City of Slaughter:*

Do not fail to note
in the dark corners of Kishinev
crouching husbands, bridegrooms, brothers
peering through the cracks of their shelters,
watching their wives, sisters, daughters
writhing beneath their bestial defilers,
suffocating in their own blood,
their flesh portioned out as booty.
And what did these watchers
cradle in their hearts?
Did they pray for a miracle:
Lord, Lord, spare my skin this day?
These are the sons of Maccabees?
The heirs of Hasmoneans
who lie in the privies and jakes and pig styes
with trembling knees,
concealed and cowering,
crammed by the scores
in all the sanctuaries of their shame?
Their pious ruses and denials are of no account,
and in the time of affliction,
on the trampled ground of the present
or on the horizon brimming with blood,
their cries, their confessions, their scourgings
will be of even less account,
fists beating against the stones.
There will be no salvation for the shamed.
And even their resignation,
their making peace with shame,
will not redeem
the cracked pillars of the synagogue

or recompose
the charred scrolls of the Sefer Torah.
For there is rot in their bones,
corruption in their hearts,
weakness in their knees,
and their bitter cry sent into the storm
of Kishinev and every Kishinev to come
shall not be heard,
not even in the porticos and corridors of heaven.

Such are the recreant Jews of the modern era.

18

RICHARD CRAVATTS'
GENOCIDAL
LIBERALISM: THE
UNIVERSITY'S JIHAD

I first came across Richard Cravatts in an article he
wrote for *Pajamas Media* on November 19, 2010, describing York University in Toronto as "a cesspool
of anti-Semitic, pro-Palestinian activism." York is notorious in Canada as one of its most prominent Jew-bashing
institutions, taking its cue from larger and more prestigious universities like UC Irvine and Berkeley that promote, in Cravatts' words, "slanted scholarship for jihad."
Genocidal Liberalism expands Cravatts' investigative sweep
to encompass the entire malign phenomenon of antisemitism *cum* anti-Zionism that has corrupted the moral integrity and academic rectitude of the American liberal
professoriate.

Cravatts doesn't pull his punches, relentlessly anat-
omizing the pedagogic bias currently in place, which is

neo-Marxist in its orientation and undeniably anti-Jewish in its expression. "In the campus war against Israel, a new rhetoric has evolved." The university, he charges, is by and large no longer "a place where civility and reasoned scholarly discourse normally occurs," given the "gradual ratcheting up of the level of acrimony against Israel and Zionism" and the Left's insistence that such criticism, no matter how incendiary or libelous, "is no more than political commentary on the Jewish state." He furnishes a near-interminable list of "strident anti-Israel initiatives" that mar the intellectual life of the "liberal" and "humanistic" university, including academic boycotts of Israeli professors, the fostering of vociferous and occasionally violence-prone anti-Zionist and anti-Jewish Muslim student groups on campus, the furthering of divestment and disinvestment from Israeli companies and companies doing business with them, and the shutting down of pro-Israel speakers.

Cravatts points to an influential 1965 essay by Herbert Marcuse entitled *Repressive Tolerance*, which planted the seed of political and epistemic subversion in the fertile soil of American academia. "Purporting to endorse freedom of expression for all," Cravatts writes, the essay instead reserved "that right, in actual practice, only to favored groups." The program "could only be accomplished ... by favoring 'partisan' speech to promote 'progressive' or revolutionary change," which would be, in

Marcuse's phrase, "intolerant toward the protagonists of the repressive status quo." By the latter, Marcuse meant classical liberal thought with its emphasis on tradition, individual autonomy, civic responsibility and limited government. Our contemporary Marcusians have learned this lesson well. In this way, the door was opened for the delivery of mendacious doctrines from post-colonial fanatics and postmodern destabilizers like Edward Said and Michel Foucault who have done so much damage to the principles of intellectual honesty and objective study on which the university is founded.

Marcuse, a leading member of the left-wing Frankfurt School, clearly drew his inspiration from German philosopher Martin Heidegger, whom Cravatts does not mention but whose spirit pervades current "humanistic," which is to say, Leftist, thought. The godfather of the current mob of academic gangsters, Heidegger was appointed Rector of the University of Freiburg in 1933, using his considerable reputation to further the Nazi supremacist dogma. For Heidegger, the function of the university was to provide what he called, in his Rector's Address, "service to knowledge" as an obligation to the National Socialist state, that is, to entrench a species of *politicized education*—in this case, the absurd theories of National Socialism, the restriction of free expression, and, ultimately, a lethal campaign against the country's and the continent's Jewish inhabitants. The current academic campaign against Jews and Israel, expressed in the condemnation of Israel as an apartheid and occupying regime engaged in the "ethnic cleansing" of the Palestinians, is merely an updated and partially laundered variant of the German original. It is a palpable lie masquerading as an apodictic truth supported by fraudulent research and revisionist infatuations. The invention or suppression of facts and the propagation of fictitious memes and venomous tropes have become the liberal academy's stock in trade.

I should indicate that Cravatts' subject has been addressed before by several erudite and committed writers who have lobbied to clean up the latrine of higher education in America. David Horowitz in such books as *Indoctrination U* and *Reforming our Universities*, Gary Tobin *et al.* in *The Uncivil University* (referenced several times by Cravatts), and Stephen Norwood's chilling *The Third Reich in the Ivory Tower* expose the academic Left's growing rapprochement with tyrannical doctrines, a symptom of its abdication from founding principles and the betrayal of its mandate. There is no doubt that the natural corollaries of the narrow, deformed and prejudicial temper prevailing in academia are anti-Jewish odium and anti-Israel denunciation. The two are indissolubly linked. Loading "cruel and destructive invective on Zionism," says Cravatts, the professors are in reality "promulgating vile, disproportionate opprobrium that frequently shows its true face as raw anti-Semitism."

Norwood, for his part, reveals how Harvard, Yale and Columbia during the 1930s embraced or were sympathetic to the fascist regimes of Hitler and Mussolini. Today, as Cravatts amply demonstrates, the educational establishment cultivates an equally comprehensive sympathy for Islamofascist themes, curricula and organizations. Third-rate thinking, ignorance, ingratitude, chicanery and political indoctrination have become the mainstays of the Humanities, Middle East Studies programs and Social Sciences departments.

As an instance of such dissembling, Cravatts directs our attention to a BDS (Boycotts, Divestment, Sanctions) manual, *Fighting the New Apartheid: A Guide to Campus Divestment from Israel,* authored by Palestinian-born Fayyad Sbaihat of the University of Wisconsin, in which we read that the divestment campaign should avoid "debating facts on the ground." In order for the BDS agenda to be successful, "Israel must be characterized as a pariah state" regardless of "specific events and facts [which] can prove illusive when one attempts to build a case around them." This confession of transparent duplicity is not only astonishing in itself, but also in its being ignored or tacitly supported by many college administrators, left-leaning teachers and impressionable students.

The BDS conference held at the University of Pennsylvania in early February 2012 provided a classic instance of the distortions, dishonesty and malevolence targeting

Israel, as legitimized by the academy. One of its principal speakers was Ali Abunimah, founder of the *Electronic Intifada* website, who is fond of comparing Israel to apartheid South Africa and Nazi Germany. Another was English professor Amy Kaplan, who went so far as to suggest methods for introducing the Palestinian mythology and the BDS campaign into completely unrelated classes in order to advance an anti-Israel prepossession clearly intended to influence unsuspecting students—and was subsequently defended by her chairpersonette, Nancy Bentley.

Indeed, as Cravatts notes, "in the past 30 years ... the Saudi royal family has funneled $70 billion into universities in the West ... to create scholarship and teaching that is almost uniformly designed to demonize Israel, advance the Palestinian cause, and undermine Western values ... while ... helping to enable the spread of Islam." Money talks, of course, but not always loudly; it also whispers seductively into the curricular ear. The scholars who benefit are "good students of the funding game." Shying away from embarrassing their patrons and focusing on the "alleged shortcomings of Israel and the U.S.," they have found a way of getting "several millions dollars dropped in their laps." This goes some distance toward explaining the prevailing pro-Arab, anti-Jewish climate that vitiates our putative Lyceums.

Heidegger and Marcuse would surely have been

pleased. As are the swarms of their disciples among the, let's say, *intellectual* anti-Zionist crowd, who have risen from the preceptorial slime and identified with America's, and the West's, enemies. The seminars of loathing they teach and promote, euphemized as "educational events," lay all the blame for the Middle East's dysfunctions at Israel's feet. And in so doing they have not only trained their sights on a pluralistic and democratic Israel while fawning before an autocratic and venal Islamic polity, but have materially facilitated the wave of antisemitic sentiment that is rising once again.

Antisemitism is not only an emotional, indeed almost glandular, disorder, it is likely the most contagious intellectual pathology known to humankind. Today, it has infected not only North American and European campuses, but has spread even to Israeli universities, many of whose teaching and administrative staff, under the convenient banner of anti-Zionism, have become willing and enthusiastic carriers of the disease. "Many Israeli professors," Cravatts observes, "veer to the Left politically and many, incredibly, share the same virulent anti-Israel, anti-Zionism sentiments." The same is true of American and European Jewish anti-Zionists "who, in a peculiar act of introjection, attempt to psychically expunge … the liberal guilt that condoning Zionism would bring upon them." The plague has become ubiquitous when even those eventually targeted for exclusion become its most ardent advocates. It is clear that a species of indefeasible madness has taken hold of the academic community.

When a civilization begins to decay and enters the twilight of its existence, it is almost invariably vanquished by an army of barbarians. This seems to be what is happening now, judging from the mental debility and cultural exhaustion that have stricken our cognitive elites. These barbarians now proliferate as an advance guard in the contemporary academy. They have almost nothing to say about any of the bloodbaths and savageries being enacted in country after country throughout the world—Syria, Egypt, Iraq, Nigeria, Iran, Yemen, Zimbabwe, Libya, Sudan, China—but when it comes to the Jewish state, with its scattered settlements in its ancient homeland and not a single Israeli remaining in Gaza or in south Lebanon's buffer zone, the chorus of revilement erupts into a veritable cacophony. The "visceral hatred by the Left," Cravatts writes, and the "singular obsession many academics have with Israel, and only Israel, from among the world's countries," is a symptom of the double standard "that has permeated the university" and "an indication of just how far [it has] diverged from [its] purpose." It is, in fact, a sign of its descent into the realms of scholarly perversion.

As many have come to realize, there is nothing sacrosanct *per se* or *inherently* prestigious about the university. Like any human institution, it can profane its founding principles and grow decadent and oppressive. The German universities of the 1930s, as we've seen, despite their long tradition of rigorous scholarship, were by no means beacons of informed thought and genuine research but propaganda factories working overtime. One must always remember that the university may as easily become a turbine of indoctrination as a generator of intellectual vitality or a transmitter of genuine knowledge.

Reluctant to intervene and prevent the creation of an atmosphere of intimidation against their Jewish students, university officials have contributed to the establishment of a hostile milieu—one that may well infringe on civil rights law. This must change or the sequel does not bear considering. But it will be an uphill battle that requires vigilance, courage and staying power. One must see that a gluttonous and possibly insatiable *appetite* for Jew-hatred has come over the modern academy. The spectacle it exhibits of unabashed relish, if not voracity, in gorging on lies and calumnies at Israel's expense is enough to turn one's stomach and put one off higher education entirely, at least as it is practiced in the socioliberal departments of our compromised universities. Professing to be disinterested and impartial, they feed on demonizing Israel and its supporters, rewriting history, benumbing their wards, legitimizing the consumption of misinformation, and making Israel-and-Jew hatred respectable.

Thus, camouflaged as nonpartisan political criticism and protected by the slogan of "academic freedom," the same old "themes of Jew-hatred are now conveniently channeled through the Jew of nations, Israel." *The rallying cry of academic freedom has gradually become a serviceable sobriquet for an academic inquisition.* At the same time, the Israel-haters, employing "academic freedom" to "proclaim whatever slander and accusation they wish against the Jewish state," do not, as we have seen, grant the same privilege or right of "academic freedom" to their opponents, whom they accuse of stifling free speech when it is used in rebuttal or dissent. "The habit is convenient," Cravatts writes, "because it means that ... history and facts can be overlooked" without having "to engage in dialogue." The intent of the anti-Zionist Left—administrators, faculty and students—is to turn an open discussion into a closed monologue.

This has led to the sedimenting of a baneful ideology which, he reiterates, has embraced the false narrative of the Palestinians as a contemporary version of black South Africans under apartheid rule and Israel as a "Nazi-like, genocidal and racist" state, a fraud that has "resonated in the halls of academe" and is nothing other than "a complete inversion of fact." It is also a "moral inversion" that has "stifled and retarded" unfettered inquiry, "sacrificing one of the core values for which the university exists." Faculties central to our humanity—faculties both mental and administrative—will be seriously jeopardized by the coarse and arrogant hospitality for anti-Jewish and anti-Israeli compulsions.

The desolation that has demonstrably befallen the academic world—the "moral dead zones where faculty do little more than indulge their basest political biases" (to quote author Michael Ross), the rupture in the fabric of memory, the intellectual disarray and pedagogic fecklessness that typify its current state of being—can be countered and repaired only by candid discussion and the recovery, hope against hope, of the spirit of integrity in individual teachers sprinkled here and there across the contemporary academic moonscape. For the university Left, Cravatts writes, has violated two "fundamental principles of higher education: academic responsibility and a fervent commitment to actual scholarship... With great regularity, academic imbecility and fraudulent scholarship has been substituted for reasoned inquiry."

A maxim suggests itself: The relation of the liberal university to Israel functions either as a stepping stone or a stumbling block with respect to academic reputability— regrettably, the latter is largely the case. "The embrace of the cause of Israel's destruction by so many celebrity professors today," writes political columnist and Harvard graduate Caroline Glick, one of Cravatts' sources, "is part and parcel of the destruction of the US higher education system." Cravatts patently agrees, concluding that the university narrative about Israel must be "reframed." Failing such rehabilitation, our universities will become no less epistemologically suspect than their counterparts in the Islamic world, as Harvard, Georgetown and Yale aspire to the condition of Al-Azhar in Cairo, Al-Quds in Abu Dis and Benadir University in Mogadishu.

It always comes as a relief to read a writer who is morally honorable, whose claims are backed by discernible evidence, whose prose is both accessible and limpid, and whose methodology is rational, coherent and conscientious. Richard Cravatts is one of this rare breed of scholars who must be taken seriously and who are thankfully not yet extinct. *Genocidal Liberalism: The University's Jihad Against Israel & Jews* makes for indispensable reading. It shows how the so-called "liberal" university has become Ground Zero of intellectual ruination, its professoriate invidiously programming its students with a left-wing, statist agenda, a misplaced tolerance for radical Islamic thought and practice and an unseemly eagerness for its natural correlate, anti-Jewish and anti-Israel execration.

Far from being the bulwark and harbinger of liberal civilization, the university seems more than willing to compromise its central purpose which, in the words of Matthew Arnold from *Culture and Anarchy*, is "getting to know, on all the matters which most concern us, the best which has been thought and said in the world; and through this knowledge, turning a stream of fresh and free thought upon our stock notions and habits." But in our sluices of learning, the "stream of fresh and free thought" has turned into a river of sludge and sewage.

Cravatts' concluding recommendations all make perfect sense, but it will be a Herculean task to get them implemented—whether exposing the cult of "Palestinianism" for the conceptual sham that it is, differentiating between legitimate criticism of Israel and thinly-disguised antisemitism, holding craven college administrators to a firm moral stand, preventing the abuse of academic freedom, cleaning up the Augean stables of Middle East Studies programs, and other such sensible requisites. He acknowledges that reclamation will be difficult, "fraught with challenges and requiring constant efforts to change long-held beliefs and deep-set emotional attitudes, but it is imperative that the task be undertaken." For it would be "morally dangerous" to permit the present situation to fester. The university must be made "accountable for its teaching and programs which deal with the Middle East, and Israel particularly." It should not be allowed to continue vilifying a nation "for no other reason than it happens to be lived in by Jews."

And it cannot be allowed to pursue its trajectory back into the 1930s.

19

RESISTING THE OBVIOUS

In much of my recent work—books and articles—I have addressed the issue of antisemitism in the contemporary world. That the beast is once again slouching, not only towards Bethlehem as in the Yeats poem, but toward Oslo, Paris, London, Stockholm, Malmo, Copenhagen, Vienna, Berlin, Warsaw, Washington, Toronto, Sydney, Caracas, Brussels, Amsterdam and many other cities and regions around the globe, should come as no surprise. From biblical times to the present moment, in their own homeland or "scattered among the peoples," Jews have never been safe. This is precisely what distinguishes the Jewish people from the rest of humanity, the specific nature of their "chosenness." Wherever they may find themselves they are always at risk, whether actively or potentially, targeted for slander, exclusion or extinction.

In developing this argument in such books as *The Big Lie* and *Hear, O Israel!*, I have been condemned by a number of my critics, who accuse me of exaggeration, self-pity or a sort of obsolescence, as if my gaze were fixed on the past at the expense of a more amenable or complex present. The fact that many of these detractors are themselves Jewish is only to be expected, for Jews have a long history of willfully ignoring the signs and rejecting the self-evident. It is not only the JINOs (Jews in Name Only), the "non-Jewish Jews" flagged by Isaac Deutscher, or the *apikorsim* ("wicked sons") of Jewish public life) enamored of their enemies, who are blind to the historical *fatwa* against them. It is also those whom I refer to as the "good Jews" and whom author and Rebel News CEO Ezra Levant calls the "official Jews" —that is, a significant number of Jewish communicants, as well as their secular counterparts—who refuse to read the writing on the wall even when it is in their own language, inscribed in block letters, and blazoned on every street corner. These Jewish critics assailed my analysis as, variously, hyper-inflated, unfair to Islam, scare-mongering, one-dimensional, and so on, as if I refused to align my perspective with the mores of the enlightened and democratic West.

But the enlightened and democratic West is no longer what it intermittently was—or rather, it is certainly not what it presents itself as being. The legacy media, academia, the political class and an alarming proportion of the public have made common cause with the anti-Israel and anti-Jewish campaign. This is especially true of

Europe whose Jewish population is increasingly under threat. As French philosopher Guy Milliere observes in *Twilight Over Europe*, "Almost everywhere in Europe, it is now dangerous for a practicing Jew to wear a yarmulke," a development that he regards as a visible and repellant symptom "of a wider and more disquieting decay." There is no doubt, he continues, "that there is something rotten in today's Europe."

Milliere's France, the land of liberty, equality and fraternity—whose 600,000 Jews are outnumbered by approximately ten times as many Muslims—is a case in point. A French Jew circulated an email detailing anti-Jewish acts of terror and vandalism in French society rarely reported in the media: "In Lyon, a car was rammed into a synagogue and set on fire. In Montpellier, the Jewish religious center was firebombed; so were synagogues in Strasbourg and Marseilles; so was a Jewish school in Creteil. A Jewish sports club in Toulouse was attacked with Molotov cocktails, and on the statue of Alfred Dreyfus in Paris, the words 'Dirty Jew' were painted. In Bondy, 15 men beat up members of a Jewish football team with sticks and metal bars. The bus that takes Jewish children to school in Aubervilliers has been attacked three times in the last 14 months. According to the Police, metropolitan Paris has seen 10 to 12 anti-Jewish incidents PER DAY in the past 30 days. Walls in Jewish neighborhoods have been defaced with slogans proclaiming 'Jews to the gas chambers' and 'Death to the Jews.' A gunman opened fire on a kosher butcher's shop (and, of course, the butcher) in Toulouse; a Jewish couple in their 20's were beaten up by five men in Villeurbanne. ... (A) Jewish school was broken into and vandalized in Sarcelles."

We recall that *France TV-2* marketed the infamous al-Dura hoax. Its Jerusalem bureau chief Charles Enderlin, profoundly implicated in furthering the scandal, received the *Prix Gondecourt* for his self-serving and dissembling screed *Un Enfant Est Mort* (*A Child is Dead*). *Agence France-Presse* is little better, taking every opportunity to misrepresent and vilify Israeli (former and present) PM Benjamin Netanyahu.

France may be leading the way but antisemitic incidents and/or anti-Israeli sentiment are on the rise in Italy, Germany, Austria, Ireland, Spain, Hungary, the U.K., Sweden, Holland, Poland and, of course, Norway. The hour of the European beast, to paraphrase Yeats, has come round once again.

It would be a serious mistake, however, to assume that America is exempt from the phenomenon. The Representing the People website, which is promoting a "Holocaust II" program, should not be dismissed as a fringe insanity. It is a symptom of the plague that is spreading. "REMOVE ONE JEW A DAY," it solicits in caps. "If every American would remove only one Jew from the face of the earth, the entire problem would be solved. Can we count on you?" On the 73rd anniversary of *Kristall-nacht*, vandals set cars aflame and painted Nazi graffiti in a predominantly Jewish neighborhood in Brooklyn. As a survey conducted by the Anti-Defamation League (ADL) indicates, antisemitic attitudes now hover at 15% of the population and climbing. (Other polls suggest that support for Israel is rising, but this does not impact a hard-core sediment of anti-Jewish feeling.)

It is no secret that antisemitism tends to flourish in times of political instability and economic tribulation, as at the present historical juncture when people ignorantly seek a scapegoat on which to project their confusion and resentment. But the truth is that it remains always latent even in halcyon periods. The sense of security that Jews have urgently sought and too often take for granted is a psychological delusion that works against an indispensable vigilance, a temptation that weakens the *sine qua non* of self-preservation. Jews who believe that assimilation provides asylum from the world's "longest hatred" —no less, for that matter, than those Israelis who believe that accommodation with the Islamic adversary will lead to lasting peace—are living in a fool's paradise.

In fact, as French-Jewish philosopher Alain Finkielkraut has persuasively argued in *The Imaginary Jew*, it is precisely the urge to assimilation that much of the Gentile world holds against Jews, even those whose "will to integration" leads them to become antisemites themselves. Assimilation is an example of "historical irony attaining a tragic perfection," for it was the very "will to integration that was really the crime." The effort to melt into the mainstream, the desire for respectability and approval, is nothing less, according to Finkielkraut, than "a bad bargain with emancipation" which culminates one way or another in disdain, hatred, ostracism—or worse.

This is the message of the *Book of Esther* (and its associated *Purim* festival), which cautions Jews that the attempt to blend in is always idle, that even a place at court is no safeguard against antisemitic malice and that Jewish identity, however inscrutable or contested, cannot be forsworn. This is true of today's "court Jews" as well, that cabal of journalists, editors, professors, authors, pundits and pamphleteers who fulminate against their own while maintaining their coveted status in the corridors of preference. One recalls how the philosopher Moses Hess, formerly a passionate assimilationist, was shocked into reality by the Damascus riots of 1840 and became what we might call a proto-Zionist.

Similarly, Theodor Herzl, founder of the Zionist movement and author of the epochal *The Jewish State* (1896), was himself a staunch assimilationist until he visited France and saw with his own eyes the swollen cloud of mindless and deep-seated hatreds let loose by the Dreyfus trial. The conclusion he came to, however painful and against the grain, changed the course of his people's history and cannot be controverted by the dejudaicized Jew who still wishes to preserve his sense of reality and ultimately to survive. Today there can be no question that, in the words of legal commentator Stephen Kruger, "The lowest common denominator of countries large and small is Jew-hatred."

American Jews, who think they are safe, should read the report titled "HKS Working Paper No. RWP06-011," first issued as a Faculty Working Paper, by John Mearsheimer and Stephen Walt of the Kennedy School of Government at Harvard University. The report accuses Israel of being a torture state, of not being a genuine democracy and of not being a reliable partner of the U.S. But their salvos are not directed solely against Israel. They then proceed to abuse influential American Jews like Paul Wolfowitz, David Wurmser and Douglas Feith for orchestrating the American involvement in Iraq and purport to show how the American Israel Public Affairs Committee (AIPAC) "manipulates the media" and "polices academia."

What is most disturbing is that this mendacious and bigoted report, which has since resurfaced in book form as *The Israel Lobby and U.S. Foreign Policy*, has the authority of a great American university behind it and, equally distressing, is only one of such numerous propaganda documents to come from heretofore unimpeachable sources or presumable experts. Gilad Atzmon's *The Wandering*

Who? reinforces the canard of Holocaust denial, justifies the libels of *The Protocols of the Elders of Zion*, and effectively blames Jews for all the world's ills. That Atzmon is himself a Jew places him squarely in the ranks of the *apikorsim*, a traitor both to himself and to his people, one of those "value-added Jews," as Nidra Poller calls them. "I no longer felt any attachment to the Jewish causes, Israel or the Jewish people," he confesses; far better to play the saxophone, to be reassured that he "might possess musical talent," and "to draw closer to the Arab sound" as he proceeds to defame Israel and Jews.

It is time for Jews to wake up and smell the viscid stench of bigotry and hatred that has begun to fill the air. What David Hume said about slavery in *Essays moral, political, and literary* is also true of murderous intentions, namely, that evil "has so frightful an aspect to men accustomed to freedom, that it must steal upon them by degrees, and must disguise itself by a thousand shapes, in order to be received." Before you know it, you are in chains. Only, as noted above, in the current moment the signs are increasingly conspicuous. The averted gaze and the serene assumption that "it can't happen here" leave a people unprepared in the face of social depravity and political infamy. There is no longer any excuse for obliviousness.

Nor is there any warrant for disowning, condescending to or pillorying the messengers who bring premonitory tidings. Worse, there can be no forgiveness for partnering with antisemitic and anti-Zionist mustelids, as did the Jewish Studies Program at the University of California at Davis, inviting Gilbert Achcar, a defender of the Nazi collaborator Haj Amin al-Hussein, the notorious Mufti of Jerusalem, to "grace" the podium.

Whether in Israel or the Diaspora, Jews must recognize that the winds have shifted once again, that appeasement is a failed strategy, that pandering to the haters or joining their serried columns will not save them in the long run, that assimilation is no ironclad guarantee against the depredations of the morally benighted, that pretending otherwise and loitering in a state of occulted nonchalance and smug indifference is nothing but the harbinger of tragedy, and that awareness, courage and the readiness to defend against assault *in whatever way that may be called for* have become necessary.

Jews must shed their complacency and take the initiative, establish pro-active organizations willing to vigorously support their cause, cease funding universities where anti-Jewish groups, a leftist professoriate and compliant administrators multiply, acknowledge that "interfaith dialogue" with Islamic clerics is a tactical maneuver on the part of a determined antagonist, know who their real allies are and welcome their advocacy, vote intelligently in elections rather than fall back on slogans and abstractions that play to their inflated sense of "social justice," understand that as it goes with Israel, so it will go with them—in brief, stop arming the enemy. For the lesson of the Jewish saga across the killing fields of history is that what has happened before can happen again. And today we are witnessing both the resurgence of an old and barbarous malignity and a growing cohort of Jewish quislings and historical illiterates.

As Ethel Wilson writes in her story *We Have to Sit Opposite*, on one level about a train journey from Austria to Germany in the 1930s, but with allegorical implications pointing to a somnolent era that had closed its eyes to the advancing dangers of the time: "Many people slept until they reached Munich. Then they all began to wake up." The trouble was, they had overslept.

20

AN EDITORIAL FROM
THE PHILISTINE TIMES

Arecent archeological discovery of a large stele at Tel-es-Safi in the Valley of Ellah in Israel, dating from the middle of the 9ᵗʰ century BC, features what appears to be an editorial from *The Philistine Times*. Known as the Moabite Stone II, it has been translated from the Phoenician by Avraham Klein and Nasim Shephelah at the Institute of Archeology, Hebrew University of Jerusalem.

~

Today is a day of mourning in Azekah. We lament the passing of our hero and champion, Goliath of the holy city of Gath, on the bloody field of Shocoth. He was a man worthy of a great people, admired for his valour, gentle nature, and willingness to die in the defense of the State. He will be remembered as a glorious martyr for the cause and will serve as an ideal to be emulated by future generations of brave young Philistines.

Standing only six feet nine inches tall, he fearlessly stepped forward, daring the Israelites to send a warrior against him in single combat. Characteristically, the Israelites wavered for forty days, unable to muster the courage to engage in a fair contest until they could manipulate the situation to their advantage.

We note that Goliath presented himself with merely an iron spear, a sword, a javelin, greaves of brass, a brass helmet, a coat of mail and a shield bearer marching before him, with which to defend himself against the ruthless and conniving David. The latter, however, was armed with a staff, a sling and five pebbles—not one pebble, not two, but five! Note as well the aggressive intent behind the symbolic number of lethal projectiles, for they represent a clear reference to the five city states of Philistia which David and his minions were determined to destroy. That only one pebble felled our champion testifies both to the unexpectedness of this low assault and to the cynicism of an enemy secretly mobilizing his illegitimate weaponry.

Need we remind our readers that the Israelitic response, as in all such instances, was entirely disproportionate? The use of a slingshot violates all the norms of standard warfare and is in obvious contravention of tacit international agreements adopted by all civilized peoples. We call upon the community of nations to raise a collective voice against the vicious perpetration of the underhanded assault we saw on the field of Shocoth.

For the purpose of this belligerent and expansionist tribe is evident to all: to attack peace-loving Philistia, crush the conciliatory Moabites, exterminate Amnon and Cush, both renowned for their tranquility and repeated diplomatic initiatives, trample the placid and amiable shepherds of Canaan into the dust, and ultimately to wipe the neighborly kingdom of Assyria off the face of the earth.

There is no doubt that the nations and kingdoms of the Fertile Crescent wish only to live in harmony among themselves, to extend a brotherly hand to the widow and the child, and to exercise the virtues of compassion and tolerance. Their armies, as is well known, are devoted to the welfare of their citizens, building bridges across dangerous ravines, constructing hospitals, draining swamps, planting crops to feed the multitudes, and assisting the victims of earthquake and hurricane. For this reason, they have been ill-prepared to meet a militant and quarrelsome people who seek only conquest and spoliation.

This is a time for vigilance and steadfast resolve against a savage and warlike nation that is also an interloper in the region. Were we responsible for their Egyptian captivity? Did we ask them to come, we who have been here since time immemorial? Are we so credulous as to believe the myth they have circulated that they were here on the land long before the great famine? What brazenness!

Do not believe the lies that tarnish the pages of the Gihon Spring Express and the Rusalimum Daily Sentinel that seek to delude those who can read. For the Israelites are the agents of stealth and worshipers of a nameless God. But we are speakers of truth and know that Dagon, most exalted of Gods, will restore us even in direst adversity.

We will carry the spirit of our fallen martyr, the noble Goliath so cruelly undone, into battle and utterly defeat the barbaric Israelitic entity. Their cowardly canniness, teeming numbers, passion for world domination, financial resources, singing of psalms to distraction, bringing stern commandments to disturb the comfort and happiness of men, invention of the alphabet and control of the means of information amounting to a monopoly on the written word, appetite for blood and advanced armaments such as polished pebbles and fibrous twine—all these will not avail them and the day will come, Dagon willing, when they will assuredly be driven into the sea.

2 1
THE JEWISH GENE?

I have long wondered what it is about the Jewish sensibility that is so internally divisive it will often jeopardize the very survival of the Jewish people in a perennially hostile world. What is the psychological factor that generates what often looks like a deeply harbored suicidal impulse, an irremediable tendency to set itself against itself, to consort with anti-Semites and even to collaborate with feral enemies who wish for nothing more than the suppression, ostracism or annihilation of every trace of Judaism in the world?

The long saga from the initial brother-slaying after the expulsion from the Garden to the war between the Two Kingdoms to the virulent sectarian tensions over the ages that would result in episodes of mutual excommunication and even bloodshed, as amply chronicled in Yoram Hazony's *The Jewish State*, to something like virtual warfare between competing political factions, defeats speculation as it defies belief. That this epic of fratricidal strife occurred, for the most part, to a population living in tenuous exile among peoples and nations that regarded so fractious and vulnerable a community with suspicion and hatred is equally bewildering.

Such a manifestation of cognitive dissonance would appear unassimilable until one remembers that the Jewish people have always been susceptible to the twin demons of willed ignorance and self-delusion. Scriptural and historical examples are so abundant that massive tomes are required to record them. Closer to our own time, a majority of German Jews refused to recognize the imminent and unmistakable signs of their extinction. The Russian *Yevektsiya* (or *Zidokomuna*) rejected their heritage, throwing in their lot with the Bolshevik revolution in which religious distinctions would be abolished, and reaped the bitter harvest. Factotum Jews have abounded in every problematic national circumstance. Even Israel itself is riven by an insidious left-wing constituency that would effectively surrender the country to its enemies. Israel's emblematic bird is the hoopoe, but when one considers much of its intellectual and celebrity elite, its self-appointed "soft" Supreme Court, its academic caste and its subversive, foreign-funded NGOs, one might substitute the ostrich.

Today in the U.S., considerably more than half of American Jews are proud of their "liberal" and "Democratic" commitments and will vote for a president who is indisputably inimical to the interests and welfare of the Jewish state and who is conversely sympathetic to the interests and welfare of Muslim institutions at home and Islamist regimes abroad. The exception to the rule was Donald Trump, who obviously did not have the majority Jewish vote. The Jewish Left has no love for Trump and, indeed, works to dilute the *Halakhic* basis of normative Jewish values and the fundamental character of Judaism itself. Non-Orthodox Judaism is dying, writes Dennis Prager, "killed by the destroyer of all good things: the Left."

Some years back I found myself in earnest discussion of these issues with the host of a Jewish convention where I was scheduled to deliver the keynote address. My host, a man of stalwart convictions, a student of Jewish history and a passionate champion of Israel, was no less perplexed than I by the phenomenon of Jewish tergiversation and self-betrayal. He had pondered this enigma for most of his adult life and could arrive at only one conclusion, namely, that there was something amiss in its genetic pool that pre-disposed the Jewish people to self-destructive behavior. He could see no other explanation apart from a toxic flaw in the "Jewish gene" to account for so irrational and perpetual a disposition to amnesia, ignorance, self-deception, and communal rupture and dismemberment. I must admit that his analysis, at least initially, seemed to me rather farfetched, but on further reflection I had to admit that he had a point. For the lessons of history, as they apply to a comparatively small and always beleaguered ethnicity which its enemies tend to regard as homogeneous, proliferate from generation to generation and cannot be dismissed except by kind of constitutional incapacity to see things as they are.

Whether this incapacity can be explained, as my host grew convinced, by a kind of genetic defectiveness, or, say, as a tendency acquired by the evolutionary experience of submissiveness, or as a common human frailty historically condensed in the activities and thought-patterns of a small but distinctive human community, must remain moot. But there can be little doubt that it exists and that it threatens to lead, despite temporary periods of abatement, to continual dislocation and suffering.

As a Jew, I must confess that I do not know what to make of my own people. Studies show that this tiny cohort is disproportionately ranked among the most innovative and accomplished people on the planet. At the same time, given its proneness to what I can only call cognicide, I cannot help but regard ourselves, by and large, as possibly the most stupid people on the face of the earth.

22

THE PAM AND
ROBERT SHOW

Some years ago, I attended a symposium featuring the notable conservative writers and anti-Jihadists Pamela Geller and Robert Spencer. Titled "The Dangers of Islamic Extremism and Western Complacency," the symposium was held at the Toronto Hilton and hosted by the Jewish Defense League (JDL). Earlier on, the Islamic organization CAIR-CAN, now rebadged as the National Council of Canadian Muslims (NCCM), had sent a brash and menacing letter to the Hilton attempting to intimidate it into annulling the event. The letter was courageously ignored by hotel management, and the event took place as advertised.

I say "courageously" since an earlier lecture by Geller, slated for the Chabad Flamingo Synagogue in Toronto, was cancelled by the presiding rabbi, Mendel Kaplan, who succumbed to the strong-arm tactics of the diversity, equity and inclusion bureau of the York Regional Police.

The bureau's director, Inspector Ricky Veerappan[1], who also happens to be a Muslim, threatened Kaplan with the loss of his police chaplaincy if he went ahead with the Geller presentation, and the good rabbi buckled.

As I strolled about the premises during the afternoon, I noticed that our national broadcaster, the Canadian Broadcasting Corporation (CBC), was conspicuously present, unloading equipment from several vans under the supervision of a youngish woman brandishing a microphone. As I had previously worked for the Mother Corp in Music and Public Affairs, I decided to engage her in an informal chat between fellow professionals. She was there, I learned, to cover a press conference to be held that afternoon by the NCCM protesting the Geller-Spencer symposium scheduled for later that evening.

Naturally, the Geller-Spencer talk was not on her agenda. It did not take long for me to discover that she knew absolutely nothing about the Muslim Brotherhood affiliations of the CAIR group, even less about the Muslim Brotherhood, and less than that about Islamic terrorism, the *Koran*, the Hadith, and the inflammatory statements of various Muslim-Canadian imams advocating stoning for adultery, wife beating, gay bashing, and Sharia law in general.

When I quoted her chapter and verse from the *Koran* mandating the killing, mutilation and suppression of infidels, she grew distinctly uncomfortable. When I mentioned a recent large al-Quds demonstration in a park near the Ontario parliament in Toronto, flying the Hezbollah flag and calling for the murder of Jews (which, incidentally, was not covered by the mainstream media), she fidgeted and said, "I'm sorry, sir, what you're saying sounds like hate speech." When I informed her that, during a previous al-Quds demonstration, two arrests were made—of ordinary Canadian citizens in Queen's Park, which is a public space, one man walking his dog (anathema to Muslims) and the other carrying an Israeli flag (also anathema to Muslims), while odious Islamic chants and placards inciting death to Jews and Israelis were tacitly sanctioned—I was once again accused of propagating hate speech.

At first, I was stunned into silence. In rehearsing the explicitly violent passages from the *Koran*, followed *to this day* by Islamic terrorists, and bringing her attention to the homicidal declarations of Muslim assemblies, I was somehow, in a bizarre twist of plain logic, guilty of defamation. I knew that what I was confronting was something akin to a medical condition common to the liberal intelligentsia, a pathological inability to parse reality—or worse, an ideological lobotomy identical to the cortical paralysis of our own Supreme Court which, in a ruling of February 27, 2013, deposed that truth is no defense in the context of giving possible offense.

Telling the truth is now understood as another form of hate speech, which means that one is no longer permitted to hate what is manifestly hateful. The corollary of this demented attitude is that one is permitted and even encouraged to lie with impunity, despite volumes of countervailing evidence, for example: Islam is a religion of peace, Israel is an apartheid state, the climate is warming owing to anthropogenic tampering, "climate deniers" are essentially perpetrating a "hate crime," conservatism is a brand of fascism, and so on, which prevarications, in another grotesque distortion of simple consistency, are not considered hateful. Such mental aberration, the hallmark of our times, is accompanied by a species of abject pusillanimity coupled with self-righteousness, a cowering timorousness before and surrender to the agents of injustice, creeping totalitarianism and militant aggression that goes hand in hand with the sanctimonious presentation of self as noble, sensitive and sublimely ethical.

This complex of moral turpitude and pharisaical narcissism was brought home to me with renewed intensity as I listened to Rabbi N. Daniel Korobkin of the Beth Avraham Yoseph Congregation introducing Geller and Spencer that evening. For nearly fifteen minutes of the rabbi's preamble, I did not hear the names of our speakers mentioned once, except when the moment came to cede the podium. But I learned a tremendous amount about the rabbi's educational and intellectual history, his great respect for Islam, his adulation of his two, late Muslim teachers at UCLA, whom he professed to represent,

and his tribute to Rabbi Kaplan—the same who had re-
scinded his invitation to Geller on the pretext, apparently,
of being in a position to do greater good by retaining his
police chaplaincy. Regrettably, Rabbi Kaplan was unable
to attend the evening's event. Of course, no reason for his
glaring absence was offered.

Evidently, it is not only the zombified media and a
bellicose and crafty Islamic cohort that have joined forces
in attacking and weakening Western cultural resolve—or
its remnant. Jewish conciliators like Rabbis Kaplan and
Korobkin, for example, or the *Canadian Jewish News* that
rejected a press attachment promoting the JDL (which,
as noted, sponsored the Geller and Spencer evening) are
equally implicated. The press attachment in question was
no doubt turned down owing to the JDL's uncompromising stance, taking to task the "Rabbis and Shul Execu-
tives bending to the Jihadist abuses and threats" (personal
communication from the JDL leadership). But toleration
of abuse, as well as the attendant unwillingness to meet
the enemy bravely and intelligently, has been a ubiquitous
court-Jewish trait since time immemorial.

As for Geller and Spencer, they were true to form,
charismatic, warm, funny, humble, factual and unabashed
in detailing with methodical precision the information
war we are in imminent danger of losing and the inroads
that "civilizational jihad" (a term employed by the Muslim
Brotherhood) and Sharia law are carving into the living

body of a failing liberal culture on the brink of moral and civic collapse. The television crews that covered the earlier Islamic conference were nowhere to be seen, though they might have learned something about the world they live in from the informed wisdom of the two speakers. Indeed, in the days prior to the lecture, the media repeated the same tedious and appeasing mantra: "The National Council of Canadian Muslims worries Pamela Geller and Robert Spencer will spread 'hate and misinformation' about the Islamic faith when they speak at a Toronto-area hotel Tuesday evening, the group's executive director said." But staunch defenders of freedom tirelessly working to repair the lesions of a commissurotomized age are either airbrushed out of the picture, disdained as inconsequential or dismissed as hatemongers, bigots, or racists.

"What we are witnessing in the years since 9/11," lamented *Freedom Press* editor Janice Flamengo, "is increasingly conscientious 'Sharia compliance' by western elites." Such "staggering illogic, inversion, and distortions … have become common currency in discussions of Islam amongst our cultural elite." For speaking truth, she was summarily threatened with legal action by the NCCM.

Adapting a famous verse of T.S. Eliot: "This is the way the world ends, not with a bang but a simper."

Notes

1. Popular Iranian director Tahmineh Milani presents a more ambiguous case. Her domestic comedy *Cease Fire*, to take one example, shows a well-off and trendy squabbling couple who could just as well be living in an affluent suburb of Paris, London or New York. Their kitchen is state-of-the-art, the car in the driveway is a BMW, and they can afford to visit a marriage counsellor—who instructs them to confront their "inner dictator." Nevertheless, the film is marred by its concessions to the rules enforced by the external dictator. The "modern" wife is never seen without her headscarf, even in the privacy of the home, and the couple never seen to exchange a harmless peck, even in the privacy of the bedroom. Milani is a fearless director who has taken considerable risks in the past, but she is hobbled by an oppressive religious authority and constrained by the need to survive. And for all its comical goings-on, the humor never really takes off and *Cease Fire* finally remains cloaked in the heavy garb of stifling religious and political conformity.

23

ISLAM RIDES
THE SNAKE

In a BBC interview on January 4, 2008, the senior prelate of the Church of England at the time, Rowan Williams, argued in favor of recognizing certain aspects of Sharia law. Muslims should not have to choose between "the stark alternatives of cultural loyalty or state loyalty." Justin Welby, current leader of the Anglican Communion with its see in Canterbury, essentially reiterates the sentiment. Indeed, the continuing rise of Sharia courts in Britain, part of an effort to turn various British cities into Islamic states as promoted by the Islamic Emirates Project, is gathering momentum.

According to Soeren Kern, a senior analyst of the *Groupo de Estudios Estratégicos* in Madrid, the UK is riddled with "Sharia law enforcement zones" with as many as 85 Sharia courts, constituting a parallel legal system. Kern cited Bangladeshi-born Lutfur Rahman, former and current mayor of Tower Hamlets in East London, who is "dedicated to changing the 'very infrastructure of society, its institutions, its culture, its political order and its creed … from ignorance to Islam.'" Rahman's dictate is gaining pragmatic strength. This state of affairs is, for the most part, winked at by the authorities. The U.K. is no longer OK. True to form, Oxford's Magdalen College has replaced its annual St. George's Day banquet for April 23, 2023 with a formal dinner celebrating Eid, the Islamic holiday marking the end of Ramadan.

It sometimes looks as if Sweden might predecease the U.K. as a viable, sovereign Western democracy hurtling into the Islamic abyss. Pat Condell delivered a memorable and chilling account of the advanced state of the country's Islamic plummet, which should be consulted by anyone who still believes that coddling the Islamic demographic is a sign of enlightened thinking, social justice and the benefits of unmonitored diversity. Hopefully, this situation may be changing with the recent election of a Center-Right coalition headed by Prime Minister Ulf Kristersson, who has vowed "to set the country on a new course on immigration."

We see the love affair with Islam and multiculturalism being pursued in Denmark, Austria and Holland where prominent individuals have been prosecuted on the grounds of "hate speech" for warning against the Islamic aim to subvert the liberal traditions of these countries. Norway is rapidly becoming a kind of earthly *Jannah* for

Muslim immigrants (Arabic for the heavenly garden, or Paradise). In other countries, parties seeking votes in the many Muslim enclaves that checker the social and political landscape will continue to "make nice."

What is occurring in Europe is by no means an isolated phenomenon. Events there will soon be appearing in a North American theatre near you and, indeed, they already have. Given the lobbying and propaganda efforts by radical Muslim organizations like CAIR, ISNA and the NCCM, the spread of Muslim influence on university campuses, and the recognition of the Muslim Brotherhood as a partner in dialogue, the die appears to have been cast. The media for its part has gone soft on the menace and is busy promoting the Muslim agenda, rarely identifying jihadists as Muslims but as "lone gunmen," of "Asian origin," or as psychologically troubled individuals. As the expression has it, terrorists tend to "get away with murder."

The Islamic fact is now solidly entrenched and continues to bore ever more deeply into the body politic, with the collusion of the Democrat and Liberal administrations in the U.S. and Canada, a significant portion of the judiciary, the press, and the vociferous left-wing intelligentsia. The European experience is being imported wholesale into our countries. Pointing this out is quickly denounced as Islamophobia. The truth is that official elements have succumbed to an epidemic of Islamophilia.

Corresponding to this love-in with Islam—schmoozing with terrorists, to quote Aaron Klein—we note the accompanying pathology of Judeophobia and the demonization of Israel in the mainstream media, the court of public opinion, the European Union, the United Nations, the majority of NGOs and the current administrations in America and Canada. This is a sign not only of collective bad faith, millennial prejudice and pure malevolence, but quite simply of massive intellectual derangement. It is facilitated by a refusal to sift the historical facts from the welter of lies and disinformation that deliberately cloud the historical and political context.

Even a cursory reading of the major Islamic texts and a modest familiarity with the historic predations of Islam would be sufficient to clarify the issue. We might say that the long-standing movement to promote Islam as a social good is proto-Woke, defined as the effort to pass off palpable absurdities and social dislocations as a forward-looking cultural development. As noted, the U.S. is not exempt. As in the U,K., its universities are already compromised. The most notorious instance involves Georgetown University, the oldest Catholic academy in the U.S., which has erected an imposing mosque, the Yarrow Mamout Masjid, on its campus. As the Muslim campaign accelerates, Dearborn will not be confined to Michigan.

This mammoth aberration goes hand in hand, in almost every European country and "progressivist" North America, with the privileging of the falsely irredentist Palestinian "narrative" that a mere modicum of applied research would categorically expose as a fiction. The isolation of Israel as an "apartheid state" is another preposterous distortion. Apartheid is in fact an *institutional* practice justified in Islamic scripture, as exemplified by the concept of dhimmitude rooted in surah 9:29 of the Koran which stipulates "submission" of non-Muslims "until … they feel themselves subdued."

What we are really witnessing in Europe, the U.S., and its outriders in Canada and Australia—the synoptic West—is the doleful spectacle of a civilization in denial, a myopic civilization that in most of its cultural and political centers will not recognize it is under attack, trapped in a defective simulacrum of what is "out there." It seems haplessly incapable of mounting meaningful resistance, let alone launching a counter-attack against an apocalyptically-inspired adversary—what Paul Berman in *Terror and Liberalism* describes as the unwillingness to understand that "a liberal society must be, when challenged, a warlike society; or it will not endure." Similarly, Michael Ignatieff writes in *The Lesser Evil* that "liberal societies cannot be defended by herbivores. We need carnivores to save us."

The inability to take the measure of a committed and imperial adversary, intoxicated with a sense of its own triumphal inevitability, is a terminal decision. The turn against reason and the civilizing imperative is merely another sign, regrettably one of many, of the West's complicity in its own demise.

24

CAN ISRAEL SURVIVE?

It has never been easy for Israel—the understatement of the century—from the day of its establishment in 1948 when it was invaded by five Arab armies to the present moment when it is facing multiple threats to its very survival. It suffers a history like no other nation in the world, surrounded by enemies, fighting wars on every front, infiltrated by terrorists, confronting the wetware dreams of genocidal regimes, in particular the prospect of a nuclear Iran sworn to the country's annihilation, and subject to an international delegitimation campaign carried out via the United Nations, the World Council of Churches, spurious NGOs and "peace" organizations, labor unions, university campuses, and a hostile European Union.

As if this were not enough, there is yet another menace it has to face, deriving from the Cain and Abel paradigm, which has inwardly corroded the Jewish commu-

nity since the thunderous instant it purportedly received
the tablets from Mount Sinai: betrayal from within. The
rebellion of Korah, Dathan and Abiram against Moses
and his mission to create a unified and cohesive people
set the tone for much of what followed in the history
of the Jews. The record is inexhaustible: the backslid-
ing tribes and their idolatrous rulers whom the Prophets railed against, the conflict between the brother states
of Israel and Judah, the quarreling Jews Josephus tells us
about who were in large measure responsible for the Roman victory and massacre in the first century A.D., the
apostates, "wicked sons" and Court Jews who have proliferated through the ages, and those who contracted the
wasting disease that Ruth Wisse in *Jews and Power* called
"the veneration of political weakness."

True, the quietist Jews who took refuge in ritual and
scripture caused no material injury, but they, arguably, in-
stilled an attitude of helplessness and defeatism into the
plasm of the Jewish sensibility—precisely what the vigorous and determined Palmach fighters and the Zionist
kibbutzniks who settled and farmed the land of Israel intended to counteract. They put the debilitating syndrome
to rest, struggled valiantly to survive and built a strong
and proud country. However, the renegades and turncoats
did, and continue to do, immeasurable harm. The motive
for treachery seems to be immemorial. As Wisse writes,
"For every Mordecai and Esther who risked their lives

to protect fellow Jews, there were schemers who turned betrayal or conversion to profit." Indeed, "the ubiquitous informer, or *moser*" is always with us. In the modern age they beget like rabbits on aphrodisiacs.

But it is not only a question of schemers and betrayers. There are many Jews who have turned against, or disembarrassed themselves of, their own compatriots for ostensibly "noble" reasons, like the *Yevsektsiya* or European and Russian Jews who joined the Bolsheviks and were instrumental in the formation of the Soviet Communist Party, until they were duly liquidated. Today, these are the Jews who vote Liberal or Democrat, validate the Palestinian faux narrative, practice outreach and dialogue with Islamic antagonists, pride themselves on their pacific and ecumenical ideology—a "universalist worldview," writes Daniel Gordi in a poignant *Commentary* essay, that "does not have a place for enemies"—and celebrate their birthdays in Ramallah bars festooned with "PLO posters advocating the death of Jews."

Everywhere we look we see these broken Jews who have embraced left-wing causes, or assimilationist fatuities, or the temptations of social prestige, or the fashionable bromides of the *zeitgeist* that promise peace and understanding with veritable antisemites in a pluralistic New World Order that exists only in their own febrile and disarrayed minds.

Their behavior is nothing short of scandalous: Reform and Reconstructionist Jews who profess to have as much (or more) in common with Muslims and Buddhists than with their embattled congeners in the Holy Land, espousing the Sabbatarian fiction of multiculturalism; intellectual and political recreants like Noam Chomsky, Norman Finkelstein, Michael Lerner, Neve Gordon, Joel Beinin, Charles Enderlin, Jeremy Ben-Ami, Richard Falk, Richard Goldstone and the contemptible George Soros who labor to abolish the Jewish state or change its character unrecognizably, siding impenitently with its adversaries; artistic Jews—I have in mind people like Amos Oz, A.B. Yehoshua, David Grossman, Daniel Barenboim, Aharon Shabtai and the late Harold Pinter, among innumerable others—who give or gave succor to the enemy; media Jews who open their op-ed pages, both in Israel and America, to Palestinian "negotiators" and avowed terrorists; American Jews who vote for the most anti-Israel presidents and who, as Isi Leibler says, have "adopt(ed) an anti-Israeli chic;" mogul Jews in the entertainment industry who tiptoe around the Islamic fact and have nothing good to say on Israel's behalf; filmster Jews like Steven Spielberg, Eyal Sivan, Ran Edelist and Amos Gitae, among a multitudinous crew of pan-and-zoom Israel bashers, who can always be counted on to impugn the nation's character or justify the Palestinians; and the endlessly ramifying Jewish anti-Zionist and post-Zionist organizations in Israel and the West that accuse the Jewish state of insensate aggression, or immorality, or original sin, or illegitimacy *ad nauseam*. As I wrote in *Hear, O Israel!*, it is almost as if there is something in the Jewish psyche that breeds *sinat chinam*, or baseless hatred, in the midst of an historic kinship.

These individuals and groups comprise a host of Joseph's Brothers who go about their business selling Israel out and, although they may not know it, are quite plausibly arranging for their own eventual misery. As Rabbi David Algaze of Havurat Yisrael said of Tony Kushner, the Jewish playwright who believes Israel was a mistake and falsely accuses it of engaging in "the deliberate destruction of Palestinian culture," he "is ignoring history and history will come back to haunt him."

The issue we are broaching is not only whether Israel can survive its obvious enemies both in the Islamic world and in the West. The same applies to its nominal friends—an Obama, a Biden, even Reagan—who claim to have Israel's back and to defend it against its enemies while acting to weaken the state, justifying their actions as "tough love." The fact is, sometimes my enemy's enemy is my ... enemy. But the crucial issue is whether Israel can survive its own. For Israel may not win through if it is constantly maligned and attacked by a swelling fifth column of fellow Jews who may bring the same fate upon the nation as it suffered in Biblical and Roman times. The Assyrians and Babylonians and Romans of yore have not gone away; they have merely transmuted into contemporary forms.

If Israel is to survive it must be defended, *or at the very least not undermined,* by its ethnic compatriots in the Diaspora and the influential cadre of its fractious and deluded left-oriented citizens. It must, as a minimal condition, be allowed to fight its wars in peace.

25

STEYN AND COMPANY:
A REVIEW

It seems appropriate to begin a review of Mark Steyn's most powerful book *America Alone: The End of the World as We Know It* by citing a mordantly unfavorable review, which will no doubt serve as a token of what any intrepid and politically incorrect author can expect to meet in the book pages of most of our major dailies. Writing in *The Globe and Mail*, William Christian opines that *America Alone* "is quite possibly the most crass and vulgar book about the West's relationship with the Islamic world I have ever encountered." After summarizing Steyn's argument that Western Europe is rapidly undergoing demographic extinction and thus colluding with the triumphant resurgence of Islam through strategic immigration, Christian dismisses the book as just another of those "rants" tailored for the American conservative market and deplores the presumably "aggressive, intolerant and radical ideology" it represents.

Christian also takes offence at Steyn's refusal to distinguish between extremist and moderate Islam. It is, of course, the noble and politically correct thing to say that the enemy at the gates is not Islam as such, but fundamentalist, jihadi Islam, and that Steyn's blanket condemnation is an unpardonable and invidious distortion. But any scrupulous reading of the primary Islamic texts would suggest otherwise. Steyn's gist would appear to be that "moderate Islam" is either the vitamin supplement of Western Islamophiles who do not wish to falter in their advocacy for the faith, or the anesthetic of practicing Muslims who do not wish to acknowledge its real nature. As Steyn reminds us, "all of the official schools of Islamic jurisprudence commend sharia and violent jihad. So, a moderate Muslim can find no formal authority to support his moderation." This is assuming that the notion "moderate Muslims" constitutes a viable category of social analysis in the first place.

Steyn has done his homework and Christian has not. Moreover, Steyn has a number of potent allies to support his thesis, such as Ibn Warraq (*Why I Am Not a Muslim*), Robert Spencer (*Islam Unveiled*), and Ayaan Hirsi Ali who, in her incendiary *The Caged Virgin*, asks: "What, then, can Westerners do? Islam is being held hostage by itself." In this view, the term "Islamic fundamentalism" is a tautology. Since Muslims believe the *Koran* is the literal word of Allah which pronounces on matters both sacred and profane and governs their conduct in the world, it follows that all genuine Muslims are, by definition, fundamentalists who, as Muslims, must consent to the indivisible unity of religion and politics. "Moderation," where it exists, merely provides the framework within which the ostensibly "extreme" forms of Islam can prosper and, so to speak, receive scriptural asylum.

For Steyn and his congeners, the distinction we like to make in the interests of political correctness between Islam and Islamism is a specious one.

Let us try to establish the context, the greater community of discourse, in which Steyn's deposition is rooted, as his is by no means a lonely voice crying in the wilderness. Prominent members of the family of ideas to which Steyn's work belongs would include Conor Cruise O'Brien's *On the Eve of the Millennium*, Pascal Bruckner's *The Temptation of Innocence*, Roger Scruton's *The West and the Rest*, Jean-François Revel's *Anti-Americanism*, David Pryce-Jones's *The Closed Circle*, Bat Ye'or's *Eurabia: The Euro-Arab Axis*, Bruce Bawer's *While Europe Slept*, and Melanie Phillips's *Londonistan* and *The World Turned Upside Down*, among others.

It is not an especially large family but, deriving ultimately from the great conservative patriarchs Edmund

Burke and Alexis de Tocqueville, with their emphasis on the need for strong communal feeling, the importance of tradition, and a robust civil society not subservient to the state, it is certainly one with an impressive pedigree. Those who are gearing up to attack Steyn for his message will, in fairness, have to widen their range of fire. America may be alone but Steyn, it seems, is in good company.

The core thesis of *America Alone* is straightforward. Steyn isolates three key factors that call into question the future of the developed world: demographic decline, the consequent unsustainability of the Western social-democratic state with its shrinking tax base and its expanding cohort of retirees, and civilizational exhaustion, that is, our way of life will stale-date in the visible future as we grow increasingly incapable of coming to grips with our dilemma. To complicate matters further, the modern multicultural state "is too watery a concept to bind huge numbers of immigrants to the land of their nominal citizenship." There is a high probability, he continues, that we are now at "the dawn of the new Dark Ages (if darkness can dawn): a planet on which much of the map is re-primitivized." The burgeoning Islamic immigrant population is gradually but inexorably embarking on a process of internal colonization to replace the aging and diminishing European population with a new "demographic profile." Islam is once again young and vigorous; Eurabia is a geriatric nightmare. As Steyn puts it, "Pre-modern Islam beats post-modern Christianity."

That the argument has been made before does not weaken its relevance. Robert Kaplan has given us the epithet "re-primitivized man," a being with a medieval mindset who moves freely among us, using a cellphone, enjoying access to the Internet, exploiting the many possibilities of modern aviation and turning to advantage the lavish welfare subsidies and favored treatment afforded by the social-democratic state. Oriana Fallaci has stressed that a civilizational war is being waged not only with guns and bombs, but with boats and babies. Claire Berlinski writes in her dirge for a civilization, *Menace in Europe*, that another Great Plague is gutting the population as the reproductive replacement rate plunges dramatically below the magic number of 2.1. As both Berlinski and Steyn point out, the United States is the only Western democracy which has barely managed to maintain the reproductive ratio, though it is sinking rapidly. I might mention in passing that there is another, Israel, which is doing even better at 2.6, so America is not entirely alone. But it is ironic to note that the demographic survival of the West appears to rest with the Great Satan and the Little Satan.

According to Steyn, America's hope and potential is that it may avoid the fate of an imploding Europe, but only if it can resist the encroachment of the kind of swollen welfare systems we see in Europe and Canada, and if it can act aggressively to beard the lion of so-called radical Islam. Nevertheless, our demographic prospects place us in considerable peril. One recalls that Ottoman thinker Said Nursi prophesied nearly a century ago in his famous *Damascus Sermon* that "Europe and America are pregnant with Islam. One day they will give birth to an Islamic state."

What Steyn has done is taken these claims and contentions, buttressed them with an array of accurate statistics alarming in their import, and tracked their logic to an inescapable conclusion, particularly with respect to Europe. At the same time, he clothes his polemic in that deflationary style, that syndicated wit some would call flippancy, that we have come to associate with his contestations, which takes nothing away from the fact that Steyn writes as a man with a staunch political conscience and equally as an exponent of common sense. All this is in the nature of satire: "he may be the most interesting satirist now writing in English," says Victor Davis Hanson.

Plainly, whether as a satirist or as a political philosopher, Steyn gives good read; his verbal friskiness only accentuates the sobriety of his themes and makes the depression that his insights induce at least partially bearable. Indeed, nobody writes quite like Steyn:

the brash self-confidence, the styptic irony, the lacerating quips, asides, and anecdotes, the unflinching engagement with the reality principle, the spry vernacular, all working together to skewer the pretentiousness of the academic Left and the saccharine pieties of the liberal intelligentsia. One gets the impression that Steyn is just too nimble and bright for the majority of his detractors, who sound increasingly emphysemic striving to keep up with his rhetorical pace. Nor, in my estimation, are they able to counter the brunt of his argument with a credible counteranalysis. Steyn's inquiry into an over-bureaucratised, highly centralised, social-welfare society, a society dedicated "to the belief that life is about sleeping in," is unrelenting. What he labels "Euro-statism," the disease from which the advanced nations suffer, involves promoting the secondary impulses—government health care and day care, paternity leave, gay marriage, cradle-to-grave welfare—over the primary ones: national defense, self-reliance, family and reproductive activity. This is what he calls the paradox of social democracy, which turns out to be anti-social. For modern social-democratic states "are so corrosive of their citizens' will and so enervating in elevating secondary priorities over primary ones that most of them would not survive even without the Islamists." These countries don't need enemies, given the depletion in their reserves of civic resolution, reproductive vitality, intergenerational solidarity, the feeling of national cohesion, and custodial responsibility for the cultural, economic, and political future. (As he intimates, the political climate will change drastically long before meteorology brings down the curtain.)

"Secondary-impulse states can be very agreeable," he concedes, for "who wouldn't want to live in a world where the burning political issues are government-subsidized day care, the celebration of one's sexual appetites," generally non-puerperal, and whether mandatory paid vacations should be six or eight weeks? But they're agreeable only for the generation or two that they last. We do not seem to realize that "for good or ill it's the primal impulses that count." By expropriating many of the basic "functions of adulthood," the welfare state has proceeded to neuter its citizens, creating an inverted pyramid or Ponzi scheme in which fewer children support more and more oldsters while simultaneously sapping their will to confront an implacable adversary. In the face of the onslaught of Islamic terrorism operating in tandem with Islamic immigration, we are losing our last line of defense: "the free-born citizen whose responsibilities are not subcontracted to the government." Even America, Steyn worries, is not exempt from the subversive temptation to capitulate. "The self-imposed constraints of this war—legalistic, multilateral, politically correct—are clearer every day" in the chastening spectacle of "a hyperpower reluctant to sell its indisputably successful inheritance to the rest of the world." This is not a question of sectoral disputes between rival cultural and religious factions or political parties, but rather of a war of attrition waged by a determined foe against feckless societies wedded to a policy of appeasement and flirting with the fantasy of harmonious coexistence. For the former, it is their century of truth; for the latter, facts suck.

"Meanwhile, we fight the symptoms, the terror plots, but not the cause: the ideology." America possesses the military clout to prevail on the battlefield and is not always shy of using it, but if it fails to carry the war into the judicial, diplomatic, economic, and informational fronts where the adversary has mobilized his most effective forces, it will be game over. Steyn phrases the American quandary in his characteristically tannic manner: "The choice for the United States is between those who believe America can take the lead in shaping the times and those who think the most powerful nation in human history can simply climb in the Suburban and go to the mall for its entire period of dominance." As for the Euro-Canadian polity— nations that cannot muster the energy even to reproduce themselves and that are preoccupied mainly with securing not their borders but their benefits—it is already the end of the line. Unless, that is, they can accept the unpalatable fact that they are their own worst enemies, labor to restore confidence in a genealogical future, and reduce their bloated welfare economies to empower the loyal, self-reliant, and productive individual rather than parasitic interest groups of whatever stripe who profit from our lethargy. Regrettably, the chances of this happening are practically nil.

Steyn's brief would obviously be rejected by the dirigiste Left as a heartless starve-the-beast policy. But it would more likely revive the human, as Charles Murray has contended in his *In Our Hands*, a tributary source of Steyn's thinking on the subject. The central argument of *America Alone*, elaborated in remorseless detail, runs against the current and will prove anathema to the concessionary thinkers of the soi-disant "liberal" West. We live in a time in which everything is fraught with danger, especially clear speech, which has the resented end of perforating the make-believe world we persist in inhabiting. As I have mentioned, Steyn deploys a direct, barbed, and acerbic language which provokes discomfort as it punctures the cherished clichés and rosy scenarios by which we run our lives, and therefore the truths he articulates must be dismissed by our teeming cadres of intellectual softies as mere "rant," as "crass and vulgar." In effect, he seems increasingly to be regarded by the punditry of the Left as some sort of Dr. FrankenSteyn, assembling his monstrous progeny in the garish laboratory of a deranged mind. But in attempting to marginalize him, they insulate themselves against the power of his critical analysis of the contemporary nanny state and the stark predicament of post-Enlightenment modernity.

Toward the end of the book Steyn formulates the credo which has dominated his thinking since 9/11: "anything that shifts power from the individual judgment of the free citizen to government is a bad thing." Or in the immortal words of Todd Beamer, "Let's roll!" It's hard to quarrel with that. It was, Steyn points out, the independent-minded passengers of Flight 93 who reacted courageously and purposefully to the terrorist hijacking, precisely what a "torpid bureaucratic culture" was unable to do as the crisis took its course and continues to impinge in a multitude of different ways upon our civic existence. Among the most urgent tasks facing us today is "restoring the balance between the state and the citizen." Improbable as it may sound, the regulatory apparatus must contract so that the population may expand and it must cease in its "attempts to supplant human judgment with government management," so that the individual may flourish. For the decadent benevolism of the modern state deprives the individual of his autonomy and thereby infantilizes him, reducing him to a supine appendage on a vast administrative organism.

Steyn's conclusion is apt. We need to man up. If

we do not recover our backbone as responsible citizens, we will find ourselves living in an invertebrate world that is no match for a supple and aggressive antagonist who has our demise at heart.

2 6

CARNIVAL AND ISLAM

Allah did not create man so that he could have fun. The aim
of creation was for mankind to be put to the test through hard-
ship and prayer. An Islamic regime must be serious in every field.
There are no jokes in Islam. There is no humor in Islam. There is
no fun in Islam. There can be no fun or joy in whatever is serious.
— *Ayatollah Ruholla Khomeini, (radio sermon, 1979)*

An interesting approach toward understanding
the dilemma posed to the secular West by so
weighty and systematic a theology as Islam may
be modelled from the work of the great Russian cultural
and literary critic Mikhail Bakhtin who, in *Rabelais and His*
World, elaborated the notion of "carnival" as an analyt-
ic category. Using his conceptual framework, we could
say there is very little "laughter" in Islam, which teaches
against "excessive laughter," however so viscous a phenomenon is to be measured. In other words, there is very
little in the way of cultural parody (or "carnival")—that

which, to quote Bakhtin, "demolishes fear and piety before an object ... thus clearing the ground for an absolutely free investigation of it," and for the puncturing of pomposity and high seriousness.

The razzing of other tribes that we occasionally find in the classical Arab *qasida*, or ode, scarcely qualifies as humor or satire, but as conventional insult and bravado. Authority is not attacked in the *qasida*, whereas laughter (in the Bakhtinian sense) is the sworn enemy of every kind of tyranny and every totalitarian worldview, whether temporal or theological. It punches holes in all the Mercators of the world laid out in dogmatic theologies and ideological systems.

For laughter, as Bakhtin writes, "purifies from dogmatism, from the intolerant and the petrified; it liberates from fanaticism and pedantry, from fear and intimidation, from didacticism, naïveté and illusion, from the single meaning, the single level ... " It restores what he calls an "ambivalent wholeness" to the psyche of man and reconfirms the festal, irreverent and material self in the face of a repressive transcendence. Or as Peter Sloterdijk puts it in *Critique of Cynical Reason*, using the word in its special Bakhtinian inflection, "laughter" is the "embodiment of that which has been negated, excluded, humbled, and declared evil. It is the id asserting itself as the ego."

This is why Salman Rushdie's sprawling and jubilant mock-epic, *The Satanic Verses*, came as an intolerable af-

246 ~ *Crossing the Jordan: On Judaism, Islam, and the West*

front to Islamic worship and earned its author a price on his head. It is the same for Islam as it is for what Bakhtin calls "the high distanced genres" in which, certainly in theory and pervasively in practice, "there is not the slightest gap between (the individual's) authentic essence and its external manifestation," whereas laughter exposes "the disparity between his surface and his center," so that "an unrealized surplus of humanness" may flow into the world to be celebrated.

A primary Western example of such grave, formal genres is the triple-cycle classical Greek tragedy; yet in the attached Satyr Play that brings the sequence to a close, the portentous tympany of Fate and the pretensions of the protagonist are subjected to the domestications of mockery and laughter. The lofty is humanized by the lowly, the unitary self by its inherent plural. Similarly, the medieval Saturnalia and *festa stultorem* reversed the established roles of Christian authority, if only for brief intervals. One thinks, too, of the traditional *Purim Spiel*—the carnival antics celebrating the survival of the Jews related in the *Book of Esther*—with its satiric plays, masked balls and general topsy-turviness making light of potential tragedy.

But Muslim monkeyshine is another matter altogether. Even the kind of mild playfulness we find in Israeli artist Avraham Guy Barchil's illustrations of the grand esoteric themes of Hebrew Kabbalah through the medium of the comic book may, in the Muslim domain, likely have cost him his freedom or more. Here it is revealing to contrast cultural modalities in the Middle East between the Islamic nations and their irritant neighbor. There is a genuinely funny and limber quality even to overtly ferocious political satire in Jewish humor, such as Caroline Glick's TV-on-Internet *Latma* routines, which could never be transposed, *mutatis mutandis*, into the cultural protectorate of Islam. But what is most illuminating as a distinguishing mark between these opposed cultural worlds is the Jewish talent for self-deprecation, illustrated and explained in Ruth Wisse's *No Joke*.

In classical Islam, "difference" is anathema and self-and faith-directed levity, an offence. Consider what the effect on the Islamic world would have been had the Monty Python film *Life of Brian*, with the lead character playing the Prophet rather than the Saviour, featured on the marquees. As Ibn Warraq facetiously asked in an article for *City Journal* (vol. 18. no. 1), "can we look forward, someday, to a *Life of Mo?*" *Monty Python and The Holy Grail* would not have fared much better either, though the Holy Hand Grenade might have struck a chord. Or how about Mel Brooks' *History of the World Part I*, with its hilarious skit of Moses dropping one of the tablets, reducing the fifteen commandments to ten, had a similar disaster befallen one of the scrolls of the *Koran*. (Brooks' *The Producers* comes very close, for all its ribaldry, to tempting the unspeakable.)

The only significant examples of filmic comedy/ satire from the Islamic world that I am familiar with are from dissident Iranian directors Jafar Panahi and Saman Moghadam. Panahi's *Offside* protests the repressive, rule-oriented mentality of the Islamic Republic via the absurdist allegory of six young girls jailed for trying to crash a soccer game. Moghadam's *Maxx* plays with the notion of mistaken identity in poking genial fun at the regime's hidebound and reactionary nature. But these directors are heavily censored. Many of Panahi's films do not circulate in Iranian theaters and it was reported in *Time*'s Europe Magazine that "the government found 140 'questionable' points" in the screenplay of *Maxx*, many if not most (or all?) of which had to be left on the cutting room floor. This is cutting satire with a vengeance.[1] Still, these films are a world apart from the Jewish self-spoofs like the movies of Woody Allen or the Charles Grodin vehicle *The Heartbreak Kid* and its Ben Stiller remake.

In Islam, submission to a unified structure of thought and worship is obligatory, fusing the individual with the collective and the inner with the outer in a seamless existential jointing. The discrepancy between surface and center, public and private, is not recognized and the prying open of the suture between the two is taboo. According to Islamic apologist Tariq Ramadan in *Western Muslims and The Future of Islam*, Muslims do not in fact "merge the categories" of the "public and private" spheres of

expression or being, but he nevertheless makes it plain
that in their relations with the world Muslims must take
"their Islamic frame of reference as a starting point." In
reality, the categories do merge. And, as to be expected,
while the index of his book lists many words beginning
in "hu," including "Huntington, Samuel," there is nothing
under the rubric of "humor."

Needless to say, despite Ayatollah Khomeini's famous radio sermon, I am not suggesting that there is no
such thing as laughter in the Muslim world, which would
be an utterly laughable claim to advance, but rather that
humor tends to manifest as a form of social levity common to all peoples or is patently non-subversive. But even
the concept or practice of "harmless fun" does not seem
to figure prominently in the Islamic mindset or prosper
as a social institution. It should come as no surprise that
the British theme park, Alston Towers, had to cancel its
"National Muslim Fun Day" on September 17, 2006, owing to lack of interest—this notwithstanding the incentive
of halal food, prayer areas, gender segregation and the
enforcement of appropriate dress codes. British Muslims
were obviously not amused. Speaking of harmless fun,
what other religious faith in the world today would imprison a schoolteacher and even call for her execution for
the crime of allowing her students to name a teddy bear
after its prophet? Gillian Gibbons might have reflected
whether her Sudanese hosts were capable of the spirit of

kindly indulgence associated with certain forms of even non-satiric humor before having exercised her indefeasible naivety.

Philip Hitti informs us in his monumental *History of the Arabs* that Arabic literature "abounds in anecdotes, jokes and remarks which to us today sound obscene," but the drift of his observation clearly points to a tradition that has been for the most part superseded, and is largely innocent of aggressive political intent or connotation. There is a tradition of critique in classical Arabic poetry, going back to two contemporaries of Mohammed, Abu Afak and Asma bint Marwan, who dared criticize the Prophet, but those poets foolhardy enough to adopt the practice usually paid with their careers and sometimes their lives, as did their predecessors. The recent attack on Salman Rushdie that left him critically injured is a case in point.

Naturally, there will always be exceptions to the rule of suppression, in the privacy of the courtyard, so to speak, and even in the media, provided the latter has been politically vetted. Take, for example, the perennial prankster of Arab folk humor, Joha or Juha (Hodja in Turkey, Goha in Egypt), a simpleminded/clever, wise fool figure à la Hershele Ostropolyer, the smart-aleck Jewish shtetl matchmaker, or the good soldier Schweik who regularly gets into absurd scrapes but often manages to turn the tables on those who would deceive him. Though poking

fun at cultural foibles, what is chiefly missing in these car-
icatural hijinks are the elements of danger and aggression
associated with the trope, the dimension of barbed satiric
perforation of the social matrix from which it emerges,
of merciless self-debunking and political and religious
pastiche. And in those cases where it is even diffidently
attempted, the consequences can be chilling. One thinks
of Adel Imam, among the Arab world's most celebrated
comedians, who was sentenced in February 2012 by an
Islamist-dominated Egyptian court to three months in jail
with hard labor for defaming Islam.

True, there have been a number of semi-satirical car-
toons in the Arab press attacking the terrorist phenomenon, but these are very much in line with official government policy which recognizes the threat to its own internal
stability. It would be unrealistic to expect anything even
remotely resembling Jeff Dunham's famous comedy routine Achmed the Dead Terrorist, which punctures terrorist pretensions and beliefs through laughter. Jokes, such
as they are, appear to be mainly of the coarse antisemitic
variety. They are probably better described as just another
weapon in the antisemitic arsenal of Islam. This would
explain why probably the most popular non-Muslim comedian in the Islamic world is the French-Cameroonian
standup comic Dieudonné M'bala Dieu Donne whose
antisemitism is now almost legendary.[1] His routines plainly do not qualify as Bakhtinian laughter.

"What Muslim culture needs," says Ayaan Hirsi Ali in *The Caged Virgin*, "are books, soap operas, poetry, and songs ... that satirize religious precepts ... Satire is a bitter necessity; it has to happen." Only, *pace* Hirsi Ali, this is highly improbable. The accumulated resistance over the ages to self-criticism and satirical reflection is virtually impenetrable, reinforced by upbringing, education, religious dogmatism, the *Koran*, the Hadith, the Sunna and *pro forma* violence. Where humor in the trappings of irony and satire may be said to exist in Islam is in the extraordinary individual, but even there it is not always as robustly developed as one could wish. And often, it must be said, what humor we may find is unintentional and should therefore qualify as bathos. *YouTube* has circulated a video clip showing an Iranian professor, Hasan Bolkhari, lecturing on the subtleties of the Tom and Jerry cartoon, proving to an amphitheater of note-taking students that Jerry the mouse in reality represents the clever and manipulative Jew. He always gets the cheese. According to this luminary, the cartoon was devised by Jewish media moguls to counter the derogatory term "dirty mice" applied to Jews in 19th and 20th century Europe. By rehabilitating the image of the mouse, the Jew was equally shriven of his murine attributes and would thus be free to continue his nefarious activities under the sign of his endearing "cuteness."

There is an absurd humor at work here which does

not originate in intent but in a kind of ablative displacement. Agency does not reside in the will of the speaker but in the disjunction from reality and common sense. The effect is not so much funny as ridiculous. The notorious Hamas kiddie film starring a Mickey Mouse character called Farfur, promoting armed struggle against Israel, including "martyrdom" operations, does not even qualify as displacement, let alone humor. There are exceptions to the rule, one such being Palestinian-American comedian Ray Hanania, who is genuinely funny. But I would conjecture that his adherence to the *Koran* and its injunctions is not particularly strong and that his theocratic devotion is tempered by the American side of his character and a Jewish wife. Another such exception may be Birmingham comedian Shazia Mirza, often billed as "the world's only female Muslim comic," whose dry humor is intended to prick cultural stereotypes. But as with Hanania, her brand of humor shows her to be influenced by Western norms and expectations and as such is not particularly "Islamic."[2]

Where such instances as Hirsi Ali advocates occur, they do not constitute an ethos so much as a deviation. The rare satirical comedian or political critic in the Arab world is almost always silenced. This is the case even in the more "liberal" Muslim countries, such as Morocco where the editor of *Nichane* magazine was taken to court in January 2007 for the felony of printing an article entitled "How Moroccans laugh at religion, sex and politics."

The charge was "defamation against Islam and the monarchy" and the sentence was a punitive fine and a two month ban on publication—a rather light getting-off in the circumstances but still no laughing matter. There are fledgling efforts like the Saudi comedy show *Tash Ma Tash* although, according to reports, it is not only Islamists who are quizzed but "liberal intellectuals" as well; even so, fatwas have been issued to prevent viewers from tuning in.

Turning to the Palestinian "territories," Omayya Joha, a political cartoonist for the *Al-Quds* newspaper in Gaza, has occasionally been critical of the surrounding Arab nations for their indifference toward the Palestinians, but since her work is almost exclusively devoted to the incitement of hatred against Israel, she is allowed to flourish. Similarly, her colleague Baha Boukhari, while suspicious of Hamas, is staunchly pro-Palestinian and something of a culture hero. There is a kind of light, underground humor in Palestinian folklore treating of sexual subjects, as in a book of folk tales called *Speak Bird, Speak Again*, compiled by two Palestinian intellectuals and published in English by the University of California Press, in French by UNESCO, and translated into Arabic, but it was pulled from the shelves of Palestinian schools and libraries by the Hamas government as *haram*, or forbidden by Islam.

Muslim raillery, when practiced in the West, is a different proposition entirely, indulging from time to time in a kind of persiflage against its own. But is it satire?

The Muslim comedy team of Preacher Moss, Azeem and Azhar Usman have embarked on what they call the *Allah Made Me Funny* performance tour, which they regard as halal entertainment. Their declared purpose is to make harmless fun of Muslim quirks and habits, thus rehabilitating the public image of Islam as non-threatening and broadly humanistic. What the comics do not wish to acknowledge is that you do not laugh at the *Koran*—you honor it or you fear it—and that any satire that probes too deeply into the cockpit of Islam will provoke a fatwa.[3] But there is probably no need to worry.

Azhar Usman is an official spokesman for the Council of Islamic Organizations of Greater Chicago and a cofounder of the Wahabbi-inspired Nawawi Foundation. Preacher Moss, a Canadian convert to Islam, is a notorious purveyor of anti-Gay jokes. Azeem, also a convert to Islam, has a background in motivational speaking, widely advertised on the Net. He is, in effect, an excellent salesman for his cause. It is no accident that the group has been approved by CAIR, the Saudi-funded Council for American Islamic Relations. Plainly, *Allah Made Me Funny*, gentling Islam via stand-up comedy routines, is only a mode of ingratiation and the obverse of carnival disruption. It bears no comparison with—to take a very recent example—Sacha Baron Cohen's send-up of antisemitism in the film *Borat: Cultural Learnings of America for Make Benefit Glorious Nation of Kazakhstan*, which, commuted to the

Islamic world, would have been taken literally and have earned its perpetrator the inevitable fatwa. The annual "running of the Jew" would not have been understood as satire had the event been billed "the running of the Muslim."

The Canadian Broadcasting Company sitcom *Little Mosque on the Prairie* is relevant here. But in a country that chuckled at such dismal, ostensibly satiric productions as *Royal Canadian Air Farce*, *This Hour Has 22 Minutes*, and the deadpan nonsense of *Corner Gas*, it seems that anything can be funny if the viewers are properly cued. The stated intention of the *Little Mosque*'s creator, Zarqa Nawaz, is to put the "fun back into fundamentalism" and to give people "a sense that Muslims have so many similarities to non-Muslims … It's the same issues, you know, a father and his rebellious teenage daughter … just because you're Muslim your standards may be a little bit different, but they're still the same issues." Well, no, they're not, and the standards are more than "a little bit different," as even a cursory perusal of local and world News should bring home. Muslim daughters often have good reason to fear their fathers for whom rebelliousness is often a capital offence.

Nawaz, who has produced a trilogy of films she calls, awkwardly, "terrordies," gave us something equally unamusing in her mosqueful of prattling pseudo-Muslims who have little in common with their real-world compa-

triots. The women on the show are cheeky, assertive, co-
quettish and adept at repartee—Western females in silky
chadors lording it over their men and parading the ges-
tures of a dubious emancipation. The clean-shaven, jeans-
clad, latte-quaffing, yuppie imam exists nowhere in Islam.
The mixed congregation is an anomaly. The bad terrorist
jokes are meant to imply that terrorism is only a media
bugbear, and the sort of problems which the little community must resolve—whether the fast of Ramadan ends
with cucumber sandwiches or goat stew—are offensively
disingenuous efforts to minimize the threat of militant Islam. And the fact that many of the sitcom's non-Muslim
characters—with the exception of the milquetoast Prot-
estant minister who rents out church space to accommodate the mosque—tend to be rather wooden and doltish
adds a layer of propaganda to this bland attempt at cultural laundering. It is a real stretch to suggest that there
is fun in fundamentalism. And it must be said that there
is not much fun in *Little Mosque on the Prairie*. The weird
silence one hears beneath the chatter and the "business"
is the absence of genuine laughter. Interestingly, there are
no Muslim actors among the cast.

The true story involves not some charming little
mosque where harmless characters traipse about trying
desperately to be droll but, as Salim Mansur, author of
Delectable Lie, has written in the *Western Standard*, a situation in which "Canada has received its share of [Saudi]

funding for mosques built across the country, where Wahabbi preaching prevails and Muslim dissidents are excluded." The little mosque on the prairie is a flimsy pipedream; closer to the truth of things is the Megamosque in London, staunchly backed by Muslim jihadists.[4] And in Canada, the real deal is the Khalid Bin Al-Wahid mosque in Toronto, which has ordered its congregants not to acknowledge in any way Western holidays and celebrations such as Hallowe'en, Christmas, New Year's and the like. According to its website, even common activities, such as watching sports programs, shaking hands with members of the opposite sex, walking dogs, etc., are to be avoided. Political activity is also forbidden except in those cases where community members are able to "exert some influence on the direction of the party so that it will take an Islamic direction" (*National Post*, October 3, 2007).

Admittedly, the proscription against laughter, criticism and the purgative function of carnival is common to all fundamentalisms. For despotic authority of any stripe, but especially for theocratic dispensations, "laughter stands," to quote Walter E. Stephens writing in *Diacritics* (13), "in the same relation to *mundus* or *cosmos* as the Antichrist stands to the *Logos*." Similarly, Charles Baudelaire deposes in *Curiosités esthétiques* that laughter is satanic in its origin and nature, something far below the "source of absolute truth and justice," hence its feral and insurrectionary power. The threat inherent in laughter is ubiquitous and is recognized and feared by credal literalism wherever we may find it.

Obviously, Western society is not immune to the many different forms that fundamentalism can take, from the totalizing dictates of religious faith and political doctrine to the general climate of political correctness in the media and the universities to the standardizing rules we find in the workplace, the school, the government, the various social bureaucracies, everywhere authorities can impose their regulative powers to implement a "universal system." Certainly, as Alain Finkielkraut has pointed out in *The Defeat of the Mind*, the postmodern Left with its multicultural pathology and sanctimonious invocation of identity politics, has become "a celebration of servitude … using threats of high treason to silence expressions of doubt, irony and reason." Like Islam, we also have our forms of cultural repression and dour humorlessness. This is the central theme of Umberto Eco's carnivalesque novel *The Name of the Rose* in which the monastic age-last, Jorge of Burgos, destroys Aristotle's second book of *Poetics* in praise of laughter. ("Every word of the Philosopher," says Jorge, "overturns the image of God" and laughter frees us "from fear of the Devil," who is necessary as a principle of social control, over both the patrician class and the rabble.)

Nevertheless, in the West the right to dissent, the comic peripety, is a basic principle—though admittedly now under attack. The right to write without censorship is, or was, sacred. The political cartoon, like the theater of dissent and the satirical media, is a veritable institution which, as the Muslim riots of February 2006 protesting the Danish newspaper caricatures of the Prophet have shown, insecure and repressive cultures cannot tolerate. The right of the individual[5] in Western society to take exception to hierarchical structures and to express his nonconformity is at least theoretically countenanced— although the prevalent tendency we have seen among Western editors and Human Rights bodies to cave in to Muslim indignation is worrisome.

Indeed, it is distressing to note the extent to which the dour and humorless nature of the Islamic lifeworld is now surfacing in the West in the form of a grim and puritanical Woke ideology, a violation of the intrinsic, Judeo-Christian creative spirit. But the option, the potentiality, is always open. The Socratic gadfly need not fear the hemlock—though he is always at risk of losing tenure, being fired, having his license to practice his profession revoked, or forced to attend sensitivity training sessions—the fate having awaited celebrated psychologist and author Jordan Peterson if the Ontario College of Psychologists had had its way. However craven our public institutions, however feeble our political will and however compromised our public morality, the freedom to laugh both at oneself and one's superiors, that is, the gift of skeptical inquiry no matter how abrasive, is a bedrock principle we cannot abandon.

When the feeling of heavy sobriety, absolute belief, collective subscription to a single master-text and devotional solemnity pervade an entire community of believers, a worldwide *umma* numbering between one and two billion human beings, we know we are dealing with a *phenomenon of civilization*, that is, with a people for whom, *on the whole*, the remedial corrosions of satire, the self-deflationary exercise of irony and the humanizing character of transgressive wit and sacrilegious humor have not been, as the evolutionists say, "selected for." Impolitic jokes, ludic inversions of unquestioned observance, derisive critiques of hierarchy, satirical playfulness—an aspect of what Edward de Bono called "lateral thinking"—are not at a premium. Acclaimed British novelist Martin Amis bizarrely feels that Islam, as a total system, "is eerily amenable to satire" but that in Islamism, "with total malignancy, with total terror and total boredom, irony, even militant irony (which is what satire is), merely shrivels and dies" (*The Observer*, "The Age of Horrorism," September 10, 2006). But I am not so sure the fashionable distinction between Islam and Islamism is a viable one since, under the aegis of the *Koran*, violence is unambiguously permitted, irony is certainly frowned upon and satire is starved out of existence.[6]

Albert Brooks' recent film, *Looking for Comedy in the*

Muslim World, furnishes a variation on the theme. On the one hand, it appears to suggest that humor is an ethnographic construct that is inflected differently in different cultures. But it also strongly implies that irony, which depends on verbal sleight and conceptual misdirection, will not readily be understood in cultures predicated on the lie, that is, in which deception is practiced as a means of survival and is the currency of everyday life. (Ayaan Hirsi Ali: "Lies and evasion play an important part in this culture … ignoring or simply denying what has happened is normal.") Where the lie has become a standard form of discourse and where almost everything means the opposite of what is said *as a matter of course*, irony cannot thrive. Laughter loses its subtlety and satire is deprived of its sting since it cannot be structurally distinguished from common speech. The armature of dissimulation is too closely shared to admit of clear separation.

This is palpably *more or less* the case in all totalitarian societies whose regimes are dependent on a subdued and uneducated populace. The swelling orthodoxy of left-wing politics and its attendant "long march through the institutions" has laid its dead hand on much of Western culture—although a parallel society of populist organizations, alternative media, widespread dissent, new currencies and economic choice have risen to the challenge. But in Islam, the *religious prepossession* tends to subvert even the possibility of lucid suspicion and adversarial skepticism which allows for ironic flexibility. Where the lie is reconceived as the truth and the truth is monumentalized as sacred and unassailable and incarnated in the Law—in the book of the Lord and not merely in the manifesto of the Leader—there is little room for Pantagruelizing, defined by Rabelais in *Gargantua and Pantagruel* as "drinking to your heart's desire and reading the fearsome exploits of Pantagruel" as he proceeds to slit the bellies of a culture's sacred cows. Pantagruelism is the cultural tipping point for any potential Islamic satirist.

As a result, the tendency is for diverse forms of fanaticism, zealotry and blind obeisance to dominate the practice of everyday life as a ruling passion. Or to put it another way, Islam as a religious macrocosm is inhospitable to the challenge of laughter and comedy, and will not readily permit the unity of its ruling cultural discourse to be fractured by the vernacular of doubt, lampoon, farce and caricature—the language of genuine subjectivity and individuation—any more than it will sanction the translation of the *Koran* from the classical purity of the original Arabic. Clearing a new and subversive space within the rigid sphere of the Law can only be condemned as a form of heresy or treachery by a bestriding orthodoxy which feels itself threatened.

For as LeRoy LaDurie explains in *Carnival in Romans*, carnival is replete with "symbolic systems" which provide "a comprehensive, dynamic, oppositional description of society," issuing in the "peccant joys" of protest against the ossifications of authority, precedence and rank. Carnival is a restructuring force with its mockery of the Partridge Kingdom mentioned in *Jeremiah 17:11* (e.g., corrupt kings, judges, priests), its overturning of the ascetic values found in formal religious observance, and its dissident representation of "the class (or clan) struggle." Through indulgence in satire, mockery and raucous festivity, carnival discharges the "flow of community…through the interstices of normative structures and ordering hierarchy" via the revolutionary upheaval of Lupercalian laughter.

Carnival, of course, may paradoxically reinforce the dispensations of normative society by allowing for the temporary relieving of social pressures, a way of letting off steam, after which life returns to normal, but it may also in sensitive times erupt in social and political disorder, as LaDurie shows happened in the small French village of Romans. The therapeutic mayhem of carnival, however, is often a prelude to social restoration, public correction and the reaffirmation of our essential humanity.

Thus ,it will be opposed by all forms of credal literalness, whether social, political or religious.[7] But in today's volatile, powder keg world, it is Islam with its billion and a half adherents, its gradual penetration of Western culture through rampant immigration, its stranglehold of the global economy via OPEC, its growing regional militancy and its theocratic retrenchment in scriptural orthodoxy, that stands most in need of redemptive saturnalia—and which it will continue to resist with the combined force of mosque, madrassa and social *habitus*.

Laughter can be strong medicine, but it must be taken in large doses to be effective, and the gelatological pharmacies are often poorly stocked. And there are always some who feel that medicine is hazardous to one's health. What Jure Gantar in *The Pleasure of Fools* calls "ethical laughter" —an initial, methodological concept—is, as he says, highly problematic and something of an oxymoron owing to its agonistic and unsettling nature, which is why it is reproved by the more abstemious school of moralists and criminalized by dictatorial regimes of whatever kidney. As Gantar concludes, there may be finally something unhealthy or unethical about satirical laughter but, unsparing and rebellious, it may also be a powerful force for the good even as it wounds. The source here is probably in Aristotle's *Poetics* where the philosopher lays it down that comedy is a representation of the people and their visceral uninhibitedness, "an obvious example being the comic mask." With this definition in mind, we might say that satiric laughter is a subset of comic laughter, a kind of verbal flanning, in that it *actively reduces* the sclerosis of high dignity and self-importance to the level of the socially inferior, to the lineaments of the comic mask.

In this sense, satire is comedy with a subversive purpose, launching volleys of laughter in a war for political and intellectual freedom, which is why it is so often contra-indicated. (If there were such a thing as the satiric mask, it would be the entarted face.) For Gantar, the vulnerable cruelty of laughter, in its lancing of the many forms of tyrannical oppression to which we are subject, must neither be co-opted nor smothered by the stolid authority of moral sobriety or the firmans of theocratic rigidity. The free individual cannot flourish in a "humorless limbo" that forbids "marginal and decentered discourses" founded in a "multiplicity of perspectives" and the cautery of ironic laughter.

It is this "multiplicity of perspectives" that is the defining element in the liberation of the spirit. As the literary critic Wilbur Sanders writes in a beautiful little book entitled *John Donne's Poetry*, looking at the matter from a subjective perspective, irony implies a "willingness to have one's feelings observed from many other viewpoints besides one's own"—precisely what presupposes an inward strength of character as well as helps to create it, and precisely what is missing from any fundamentalist creed.

Ultimately, irony is good for the fitness of the soul: it has iron in it.[8]

Notes

1   Many of Dieudonné's routines, like dressing up as a rabbi and crying "Isra-heil" or, in a particularly virulent anti-Israel number, impersonating Hitler in his bunker and claiming that "in the future people will come to realize that I, Adolf Hitler, was really a moderate," are much appreciated by antisemites everywhere, but he has become something of a culture hero to French Muslims.

2   Flying El Al to Israel, Hanania quipped that he knew he was on an Israeli airline when the toilets said "occupied." But neither does he spare Palestinian sensibilities. "We Palestinians screwed up. We gave this country the wrong name. Feinstein, Einstein, Palestine." According to Hanania, the Middle East "road map" to peace must fail since Israeli and Palestinian men are such terrible drivers. Mirza also has her moments, but anyone who in a comic routine performed shortly after 9/11 can joke, even in the effort to establish the innocence of the larger community, "My name is Shazia Mirza ... at least that's what it says on my pilot's license," must give us pause.

3   So far as I can tell, there is little or no humor in the *Koran*, which is one of the ways in which it differs from the Bible. Abraham's bargaining with God reads almost like a comedy skit and the parables and aphorisms of Jesus are filled with humor, parody and irony.

4   The mosque is supported by the Islamic radical movement, *Tabligh-i-Jamaat*, originating in the extremist Deobandi sect that also gave us the Taliban. *Little Mosque on the Prairie* is like a preschooler's finger painting. A far more accurate picture of the Muslim reality is furnished by British TV Channel 4's *Dispatches* program, whose *Undercover Mosque* segment, aired on January 15, 2007, disclosed the painful truth. London is the West's Islamic future. One need only look at the Regent Park Mosque, the Saudi-backed London Muslim Centre and the notorious Finsbury Park mosque and their involvement in terrorist activities. Again, in a real-world situation, minister Donald McKay of the Campbell Baptist Church in Windsor, Ontario, unlike his counterpart in the sitcom, had to revoke an act of interfaith hospitality. Having scheduled three speeches to be given on church premises by former Muslim terrorist Zacharia Anani, who argues that the roots of violence are planted in the *Koran* and cites a bordereau of relevant passages to substantiate his point, pastor McKay was forced by the uproar that ensued to cancel

the last two lectures. "It's hard to believe we're in Canada," he said afterward, "I feel like I'm in an oppressive regime ... I think our liberties are being eroded ... if something is not said, we're all going to be under sharia law in 15 years." This is the reality that innocuous fustian like *Little Mosque* works to camouflage. The hit TV series *24* also hews closer to our real concerns than does the CBC sitcom. For the Muslim community in the West, the problem is not negotiating a lease to establish a user-friendly mosque in Mercy, Saskatchewan but to prevent a nuclear suitcase bomb from detonating in Valencia, California.

5 In *The Temptation of Innocence*, Pascal Bruckner says of the concept of the individual that this "ideal must be constantly held up to the various counterfeits that circulate today under the name of individualism," which for most of us who aspire to this distinction is really "only a series of lapses, of escapes into cowardice, routine, and subservience." True individualism is to be understood as structured like a "pioneering experiment conducted by exceptional personalities who dared to emancipate themselves from prevailing dogmas and practices ... " In the last analysis, a faltering individualism "will not be cured by a return to tradition or by increased permissiveness but by a more demanding definition of its ideal ... "

6 There is no real distinction between Islam and Islamism, as Amis implicitly admits when he considers what life would be like under an Islamic Caliphate. Such an imperium would introduce us into a world "of perfect terror and perfect boredom, and of nothing else—a world with no games, no arts, and no women, a world where the only entertainment is the public execution ... Islam is total ... Indeed, there is no individual; there is only the umma—the community of believers." Perhaps Turkish president Recep Tayyip Erdogan said it best: "There is no moderate or immoderate Islam. Islam is Islam and that's it." This is not a world in which humor, irony and satire may be expected to blossom. The Borg do not laugh.

7 In a cogent article for the *National Post* of February 8, 2006, entitled "They don't get it," Barbara Kay points out that while, in the West, "satire is a vehicle for moral, social and political correction," public shaming "can't work on a target that doesn't 'get' irony…we forget that irony is a peculiarly Western critical marinade, flourishing in societies that value the unfettered freedom of reason and the imagination. Irony is not understood by solipsists and is viewed as a

subversive element by totalitarian regimes." Thus, it must "wither[
] among the literalist flock serving unitary ideologies like Communism or doctrinaire Islam." Satire, she concludes, correctly, is only
effective "when its target is capable of modifying the behavior the
ridicule throws into relief ... But where no correction is possible,
there is no humor." The formula works in reverse as well.

8   Methodologically speaking, satire is a literary genre and irony a
rhetorical trope, but for the purposes of this essay the two terms are
used more or less interchangeably to indicate a habit of mind.

Printed in the USA
CPSIA information can be obtained
at www.ICGtesting.com
LVHW021253020124
767820LV00015B/684/J